LARRY DANN

Oh, What A Lovely Memoir

DEVONFIRE

OH, WHAT A LOVELY MEMOIR
By Larry Dann

First edition published December 2023 by Devonfire Books

Cover and spine design by Oliver Crocker

Project editor and internal design by Oliver Crocker

Proofread by Tessa Crocker

ISBN 978-1-8382819-4-6

Copyright © Larry Dann and Oliver Crocker, 2023

The moral right of Larry Dann to be identified as the author of this work has been asserted in accordance with the Copyright, Designs and Patents Act 1988.

All rights reserved. No part of this publication may be reproduced, stored in or introduced into a retrieval system, or transmitted, in any form, or by any means (electronic, mechanical, photocopying, recording or otherwise) without the prior permission of the publisher. Any person who does any unauthorised act in relation to this publication may be liable to criminal prosecution and civil claims for damages.

Any comments made in this publication remain the opinion of those making them and do not necessarily represent the views of Devonfire Books or any affiliates.

The photographs featured have either been supplied with permission or come from the author's personal archive and every effort has been made to credit and acknowledge accordingly.

Printed and bound by 4edge Limited, UK

This book is sold subject to the condition that it shall be not, by way of trade or otherwise, be lent, re-sold, hired out, or otherwise circulated without the publisher's prior consent in any form of binding or cover other than that in which it is published and without a similar condition including this condition being imposed on the subsequent purchaser

For Liz

Contents

Introduction by Brian Murphy		2
1.	A Family At War	3
2.	A Knock At The Door	13
3.	Living At No. 7	21
4.	I Did It My Way	31
5.	Coming Of Age	43
6.	The Day That Changed My Life	59
7.	Joan's Army	71
8.	Living In America	79
9.	The Swinging Sixties	91
10.	Hitting The Big Time	105
11.	The Road To Rutherford	121
12.	Let Me Tell You A Story	133
13.	Lady Luck	143
14.	Carrying On	155
15.	Brushes With The Law	167
16.	Empty Your Pockets, Son	177
17.	My Sporting Life	189
18.	Roger, Over And Out	199
19.	A Year To Forget	211
20.	An Actor Retires...	221
21.	The Golden Years	235
Acknowledgements		248

INTRODUCTION

By Brian Murphy

I first met Larry Dann in 1962, when he successfully auditioned for Joan Littlewood's Theatre Workshop at Stratford East. At that time it was not only needful for an actor to have talent, but also to possess generosity of spirit and willingness to assist in all aspects of a production – to be a team player. The young Larry proved to have all these qualities and was welcomed aboard.

    I worked alongside Larry as an actor, and sometimes a director, over many years, and always felt confident for the success of a production when he was part of the company.

    Larry went on to have an exciting career in television as a long running character in the hit police drama *The Bill*, amongst many other programmes, and also appeared in a number of the iconic *Carry On* films, stories of which are told in this autobiography, which I hope you enjoy.

CHAPTER 1

A Family At War

I made my grand entrance into the world on May 4th 1941, at ten minutes to midnight, during an air raid. Eleven minutes later and I would never have been able to use the famous *Star Wars* quote on my birthday over the years. If you don't understand that reference, have a look on Google or ask a young person! I was born at Queen Charlotte's Hospital, which was based down the Hammersmith end of London's Goldhawk Road for over 250 years, before eventually relocating to more modern premises. My mother recalled that as bombs were falling close by, all the newly born babies were taken from the ward to a place of safety. Once the 'all clear' had been given, the mothers were all sent to collect their newborns and take them back to the ward. My Mum insisted that she picked up the right one, though I have never been sure!

My Mum, Barbara Elizabeth Forbes, was born in Southall Road, Acton on 19 February 1917. She was eldest of six children, with Ian, Margaret, Brenda, Donald and Jean eventually making up the rest of the family. Her mother, Helen Morrison, was born on 27 July 1894 on a farm in the small village of King Edward, near Buckie in Scotland. Nan would marry another Scot from the area, John Forbes. They later moved to London, where John was a chemist and owned a shop on Leinster Road in Bayswater. By all accounts, the shop was fairly upmarket and did very well. My Mum recalled that her parents lived a good life, attending parties, dances and formal dinners with the 'well to do'. Whilst they attended these functions, Mum would be left in charge of her siblings. All the children were disciplined to the extent that "children should be seen but not heard".

I later found out that in 1934, John Forbes committed suicide. The coroner determined that he had died from an overdose of a drug. The coroner gave an open verdict, but the family knew what he had done. As my grandfather was a chemist, it would have been easy for him and he would have known what he was doing, but why did he take his own life? My Mum would have been 17 when this happened and she never spoke of this, nor did my Nan. From what I have been able to piece together, it seems that he had a big gambling problem and lost the lot, including the chemist shop. Apparently he also suffered from aggressive piles. It was a sign of the times that my parents never talked about personal events, though looking back as I write this, I now realise my dreadful habit of not asking them for the answers to my many unanswered questions. I should have tried harder.

After the tragedy of losing her husband, Nan sent Margaret to live with a friend of hers, known to all as 'Auntie Floss'. I believe the rest of the family stayed together as they moved from pillar to post. Nan later met and married Bill Norton, an Australian from Launceston, Tasmania. The family then moved to 36 Wellesley Road, Chiswick, where they lived on the first floor. The flat had three bedrooms, a kitchen living room and a bathroom. Nan later let out the two small bedrooms, one to a milkman and the other to a man who worked at Diamond H Controls. I would get to know No. 36

very well and recall that it had a large garden with many fruit trees, where we had our pick of plums, pears, apples and cherries. Bill looked after this garden, as the occupiers of the two flats downstairs were old ladies! Bill very quickly became my 'grandfather'.

One of my earliest memories is playing in that garden with my Uncle Donald, who was the youngest of my Mum's siblings. Known as 'Nipper', Donald became my godfather and was a very good cyclist who used to compete in six-day races. Unbelievably, each two-man team would cycle continuously, 24 hours a day, taking turns in relay fashion. Sadly, Donald died on 8 March 1945. He was a rear gunner in a Wellington that was shot down over the Channel, just three months before the war ended; another nightmare for the family. Fortunately, the rest of my Mum's family all survived the war and I later got to know my aunts and uncle, all wonderful people, very well.

Mum's sister Margaret married Bill Kelly and together they set up a jigsaw factory, starting in Luton and later moving to Stonham Aspal in Suffolk, where it became very successful. They had four children; Dennis, Barbara, Rita and Diane. Her sister Brenda later married Len Dawson and they lived in Ashford, Middlesex, where they had three children; Sheila, Geoffrey and Linda. Mum's youngest sister Jean would marry John and they lived in Chichester, where John ran a grocer's shop. They eventually moved to Stonham Aspal where John worked for the Kellys at the jigsaw factory. They had four children; Carol, Michael, Joyce and David.

Of all my Mum's siblings, it is perhaps my uncle Ian who I got to know best. Ian became very successful when he joined Mobil Oil, where he rose through the ranks very quickly, eventually going to work for them in the USA. Ian was a very popular man and I had many a great time with him, as he used to take me to Chelsea and Lord's. I think he treated me as his proxy son. He had a daughter, Ryma, and was married to Dorothy, who was known as 'Auntie Ditty', a lovely lady who lived to the ripe old age of 99. Ian sadly died in his sixties, spending his final days with Ditty in Bournemouth. I didn't visit them often enough.

I have very few memories from my childhood during the war and my Mum never really told me what was happening in our lives. Mum's youngest sister Jean later told me that she looked after me a lot, as Mum was working as a specialist 'tinter' in an up-market ladies hairdresser called Antoine's at 38 Dover Street, just off Piccadilly at Green Park. I have vague memories of going there, where Mum had clients ranging from film stars, minor royalty and wives of lords. Jean also told me, with some jealousy, that as a result Mum had a very good social life and I was therefore farmed out to whoever could take me. I have photos to confirm that Mum was a very beautiful woman, therefore I have no doubt this is why she could have a 'good' time during the war. I understand that George Raft, a big film star of the day who was also known to have associations with the underworld, asked her out to dances. I believe she went too. She did tell me that once she ran to catch a bus, but that she just missed it. Moments later, Mum watched in horror as she saw that bus get hit by a bomb!

I can remember listening to the bombs falling from the air raid shelter in the garden at my Nan's house in Wellesley Road. I also have a memory of being left with a young girl at what I thought might be a safe house away from London. I did approach Mum about this, but was assured that this did not happen. But I know I was there a while, possibly aged three at the time. A savings book was opened for me at a Post Office in Madeley, Crewe, but I never got an answer as to who opened it or why. I do know that a family called the Monalescues used to look after me in Chiswick, as I later found out by being at school with their daughter, Marcia. I also remember being down the cellar of my Dad's father's barber and tobacco shop at 517 Chiswick High Street, where you could hear the sound of the siren screaming from the petrol station just across the road.

I have no memory of my Dad during the war, as he was away fighting the Germans, not returning until 1946. And in all honesty, I really don't know too much about his family history either. His father, Christian, apparently had no birth certificate, but we believe that he was born in 1873. I remember my grandfather taking me fishing, something I didn't enjoy, but he had bought me a fishing rod with all the accessories, so I did the honourable thing and kept trying. I think he must have become aware of my disinterest and so only took me a few times. I don't remember my father ever being with us, nor can I recall where we went to fish. As the family didn't have a car, and as Christian's shop was near Kew Bridge, perhaps we fished along this part of the river Thames.

I was about ten when Christian died at Springfield Hospital in Tooting, apparently from 'fish poisoning', which was reported in the papers. He left all his grandchildren a share of his estate and I got £90, though I wasn't allowed to have this until I was 18. Dad opened a bank account for me with this and encouraged me to try and save. £90 was quite a lot of money in 1951, though not so much by the time I could use it in 1959. When I later asked Dad about his father's background, he said he didn't know, as he had never been told! He thought that he was born on Heligoland, a small island in the Baltic, just off

Germany. The surname Dann could well be German, or if it was shortened from Dannenberg, it might perhaps be of Jewish origin? I have tried to find out more information, but sadly Heligoland was heavily bombed during the war and the archive where all the records were kept was totally destroyed. My Dad never spoke of his mother, Rosa, who died in 1944. From what I have been able to find out, Rosa was apparently a harridan with a temper not to encourage.

My father was never forthcoming with information about his past, but I do know that Norman Leslie Dann was born on 28 October 1915 in Plumstead, Southeast London. He was the youngest of six children, the eldest being Hubert Christian Dann, known as 'Sonny', who was nearly twenty years older than my Dad. I never met Sonny, or Dad's sister Edna and sadly neither did he, as she passed away before he was born, at just 10 years old. I did get to know his three other sisters, the eldest two being Doris and Vera, who was known as 'Teazer' and lived just off Hounslow Heath. I spent a lot of time there playing with her four children, Geoffrey, Dennis, Bobbie and Sally. Teazer reminded me of my Nanny Norton, as they both loved a game of cards. I never saw her husband Edward, who would go upstairs whenever we arrived, and then when we weren't looking he would eventually sneak off and go out…

The youngest sister was Joyce, who was the sibling that my Dad was closest to, as she was only a couple of years older than him and they were both many years younger than the rest. It was Joyce, along with her husband Reg, whom I would get to know the most from my Dad's family. Joyce and Reg took over my grandfather's barbers and tobacconist shop after he died, though they changed it into a ladies' hairdressing salon. Reg was a fine builder who had trained as a master plasterer and he turned the shop into an amazing place. The theme of the salon was tropical and they decorated it with palms and bright colours. It became very popular and did excellent business, meaning that they soon opened a second salon in Hounslow.

Fate fell on them however when the Chiswick flyover was proposed. The shop was smack bang in the middle of it and a compulsory purchase order was made and they were bought out at what I understand was a very low price, nowhere near its real value. They sold their other shop in Hounslow and moved to Mevagissey in Cornwall, where they bought a large house that Reg turned into an upmarket guesthouse called Valley Park. The huge garden had an orchard and palm trees, and Reg built a large pond. I would spend many happy times with Joyce and Reg when they lived there.

At first, it seemed quite incongruous to me that Joyce and Reg would run a guesthouse. Reg was not an especially sociable human being and Joyce's classy manner made me assume that she might have thought the idea of serving breakfast and tidying up after their guests was beneath her. But they did it well and again this business was very successful. Though the time came, as it often did for them both, when they became fed up with Valley Park and sold it, probably at a loss. They then bought a large property on the harbour front that had been a fish-smoking factory. I wondered about the change, but Joyce had these ideas and Reg carried them out. Joyce wanted to turn this old factory into a very upmarket coffee shop, which would seat forty customers and would serve up posh things for the time, like filter coffee and various teas and cakes that had never been seen in Cornwall before.

With very little help and in only six months, Reg turned this run-down building into a very fine establishment. He was an amazing man and could do anything when it came to building. He once showed me how to hit a six-inch nail into a piece of wood with the palm of his hand! He did wrap a handkerchief around it, but I was wincing as he did it. There was not a mark on his palm after this extraordinary display, though he made me promise that I wouldn't tell Joyce! They named the coffee shop The Wheelhouse and the building is still there to this day. But it wasn't long before once again they lost interest in this venture and sold it, I believe at a low price, because of their wanderlust. I seem to recall they created another smaller guesthouse near Probus in Cornwall, and then another near Stonehenge.

It seemed their whole life was to build and move on, which is perhaps why they never made the money they should have done. After at least ten projects, they finished up in a very small house in Gosport in Hampshire, where Reg died not too many years later. Auntie Joyce then moved back to Devon and lived in a small flat in Dawlish, before eventually having to go into a home. When she passed away, there was very little in the bank. I was always fascinated by them as a couple; one had great visual ideas and the other knew how to construct them. It just always seemed like such a shame that they had left so many of these super properties and finished up in a home that, in their earlier days, they wouldn't have given a second glance.

But what of my father and his early days? My Dad was very bright and passed all his exams and could have gone to Oxford, but I suppose the family couldn't afford to send him there. Christian needed him to earn a crust to help the family and so he got a job at Harrods in the furniture department. When war broke out, he enlisted in the Army, eventually becoming a major. Apparently he specialised in the transport side, sorting out Jeeps and other vehicles. When the war ended, he stayed on in Berlin for at least a year to work on repatriation. Returning home he was back at Harrods and after a time he became chief buyer.

As far as I know, Dad only had one friend, a gentleman known as 'Mac', who also worked at Harrods in the Optical department. My parents couldn't have been further apart in their social lives. Dad rarely had a drink and I think the first time he ever went to the theatre in his life was to eventually see me in a play. Mum had hundreds of friends and she liked a drink. She also took part in amateur drama, performing in plays at Chiswick Town Hall. So what was the attraction between my parents? I don't actually know how they met, but I am led to believe that Mum had married Dad because he was going to war and she thought it might be the best thing to do, as she might not see him again. I believe that this was the cause of many a marriage at that time. Although he went off to war in 1939, he must have had leave in September 1940, at which point he presumably returned and did the deed, as this must have been when I was conceived.

It wasn't until many years later, after they had both died in fact, that I gathered up all their memorabilia from the past and discovered letters that opened my eyes. It was Dad's stuff that surprised me most. Apparently during his time serving in Berlin, he had an affair with his German secretary and wrote to Mum asking for a divorce. He also wanted me. Mum refused and when he eventually came back to England it was only then that he basically started the marriage with Mum. War makes strange bedfellows. I had no knowledge of any of this until after they had both passed away. So many things started to fall into place about our life as a family, as I can't remember either of them saying to each other, or to me, the words 'I love you'. I also don't remember them ever celebrating their wedding anniversary; they got married in January 1940, but I don't know which date exactly. Not long after Dad had returned in 1946, we moved into a new home, which is where my own memories really begin…

Mum acting in an amateur theatre production *(Author's Collection)*

CHAPTER 2

A Knock On The Door

In 1948, we moved into No 7 Burnaby Crescent, a large four-bedroom Victorian house in Chiswick, which Dad rented for, I'm sure at the time, a paltry sum. Heaven knows what it would cost today, as the houses on this street now sell in the region of £2,000,000! It was only now that I was really starting to get to know my Dad. After the Second World War, he was seconded to Berlin as part of the repatriation organisation that tidied up the paper work for refugees, something that by strange coincidence I would end up doing in a film much later in my career. I know Dad came back to England many months after VE Day. He would never speak to me about what he did, or even where he was based for the duration. I did ask the obvious question that a young boy would be most curious about… "How many Germans did you kill?" Unsurprisingly, this tactless question did not receive an answer!

Dad worked a six-day week at Harrods, so it must have been on a Sunday afternoon in the early summer of 1948 that there was a knock on the door. My Dad answered and chatted with a man on the doorstep for a while. This man turned out to be Derek Knight, who had served in the same regiment as my Dad. The front door closed and Dad went to speak with Mum about the conversation he had just had. They then asked me to come into the front living room. This was unusual, as we only used this room for special occasions when we had guests. I vividly remember, as I walked towards the front room, thinking to myself "What have I done to this man? Have I upset his family? What had he told them?" Dad came straight to the point and asked, "Do you want to be in a film?"

I honestly didn't know what they meant, which they understood by my obviously blank expression. They explained that I had been asked to go to a studio for a day to be in a film. Fortunately, as it was during a school holiday, they said I was allowed to go if I wanted to... Wow! Be in a film? I had never even seen a film, as I was not yet allowed to go to Saturday morning pictures. So the idea of being in one, at just seven years old, was very exciting. This was to be an adventure!

I was amazed that my Dad had agreed to this, though obviously Mum was the instigator of this decision, as she was the keen amateur actress. As her only son at the time, she was keen for me to follow in her footsteps. Sadly, I never saw her perform on stage, because by the time I was old enough to go, she had three more sons to look after and was far too busy to have acting as a distraction.

The day came and there I was at 6am waiting outside 26 Wellesley Road in Chiswick, which is where Rona Knight, the principal of the Corona Academy, lived with her mother, who became known to us all as "Old Mrs Knight." The Corona Academy was founded in 1950 by Rona and her sister, Hazel Malone. They had previously formed a singing and dancing group called 'Corona Babes', which performed professionally all over the country in the 1930s. In fact, my Auntie Joyce had been a Corona Babe. Rona never married; her fiancé had been killed in the Second World War and I don't think she ever got over it. She never spoke of her private life, but I somehow gleaned facts over the years. It was because of this loss, I think, that she then dedicated the rest of her life to teaching theatre studies.

Hazel had married an Irish singer-entertainer called Danny Malone, who had left her with a son, Cavan. I have no idea what happened to Danny; like her sister, Hazel never discussed her private life with me. Having started as a teacher at the Academy, Hazel had now given this up and opened an agency for children to appear in films. This agency was based at 26 Wellesley Road, which is where my Mum had escorted me to for my 6am call. This was a five-minute walk from our home and we walked past my Nan's house at No. 36 on the way. The front door opened and after I said my goodbyes to Mum, I was ushered into the hall, where there were a quite a few boys already inside, none of whom I knew. Fairly soon, the hall was full of seven-year-olds.

We were then told to get on the coach, which was waiting to take us to Denham Studios. The journey must have taken over an hour in this bone-rattler of a coach. I was aware that many of the boys were old hands at this game, where I of course had no idea what was to happen. When we arrived at the studios, we were taken to what was to be our dressing room; the first of many hundreds I have frequented over the course of my career. We had two chaperones, one of whom was Hazel, while the other was the sergeant major of all chaperones, Gladys Gowans. I will never forget her. We were terrified of doing anything that might upset her, as she had a face that would sink a thousand ships. I was told by one of the boys that she had the power to have you sacked from the film if you misbehaved. I can't remember if we had a person from Wardrobe to check whether what we were wearing would work for the scene we were about to appear in. I remember thinking that it wasn't much fun so far, but it was already a lot better than double English lessons with Mr Lowe, my least favourite teacher at school.

Everything changed when we were taken to the 'set'. I was hit by the smell of the studio, which I can still grab from my memory now. It was a fantastic smell, which is so difficult to describe, but it was like a combination of pungent dust mixed with the recently applied paint on the set walls, both heated by the huge lights that hung from the rafters. Then throw in the added smell of the many sweaty people who were working hard on the floor doing their various tasks. It sounds disgusting, but it was an unforgettable aroma and I felt I was in heaven.

The studio was huge and we were all seated in a corner, where Mrs Gowans made sure we sat correctly as we waited for our 'call'. All I could see at that moment were the backs of canvas flats and I still had no idea what we would be doing. It wasn't long before we were called onto the set where we were to be filmed. It was a classroom! I couldn't believe it, I had not long left one for my summer holidays and here I was sat at a desk in the middle of another! We sat there for ages whilst this huge camera was moved about and lights were positioned, mainly directed at a lady sitting at the teacher's desk. This lady wasn't the lady who eventually came in to say the dialogue; the role was being fulfilled by her 'stand-in'. I was already learning about the ways of filmmaking! The sound department had a huge 'boom', as it is known, which was a microphone attached to an expanded arm, mounted on a large four-wheeled platform with a man to control it. A tape measure was used to measure the distance from the camera to the 'stand-in' lady. I wondered why no one wanted to measure me? There seemed to be a lot of shouting between a man on the ground to a man up in the gantry. This 'setting up' might have taken a long time, but I was excited about the process. I knew at that moment that this was what I wanted to do.

Then once everything was set up, the stand-in lady playing the teacher was dismissed and another lady came in and stood in her place, where she was taken through her lines. Then a gentleman called Harold French, who I now know was the director of the film (thanks IMDb) chatted to us about what we were supposed to do. I have no idea what he said to us, as I was too busy taking in all the activity around me. The actress started her dialogue, which seemed to be about the lesson we were supposed to be deeply interested in, and then a man came into the room to chat to the teacher, before he then left again. This was repeated a few times and then we were all told to "get ready for a take!"

More activity occurred as various new faces appeared, who were mostly occupied with the actor and actress, fussing all over them. A loud bell sounded, followed by screams of "Quiet on set!" For a moment there was complete silence, before a call of "Turnover…" Then after another short burst of silence, came a reply of "Speed", swiftly followed by "Action!" This process was to become very familiar to me; a ritual I would see performed thousands of times throughout my career. I'm not sure how many takes were done on this set up, but after a while us kids were asked to leave, whilst the camera was moved so as to shoot the scene again from another angle. This was the most boring part, as it took ages for everything to be moved.

Once again us kids were sent to our corner of the studio, sitting upright in our chairs. Mrs Gowans came into her own at this time, behaving like a sentry on guard at a prisoner of war camp. Many of the boys who were experienced at this game had brought along comics and books to read. I had nothing and I hadn't really been accepted as one of the crowd yet. The time passed so slowly when all I could do was sit still with nothing to do, all while Sgt Major Gowans was on patrol.

I'm not sure how, but at some stage I managed to get away from her and I began to wander around this very large studio. I found myself behind the set where we had just been filming and I came across the lady who was playing the teacher, with the man who was with her in the scene. They didn't see me, but I saw them… and they were kissing! It wasn't until possibly twenty years later when I finally saw the film, which was called *Adam and Evelyn* and I realised that during my daring escape from Sgt Major Gowans, I had stumbled across Jean Simmons and Stewart Granger, sharing an embrace. This was before they were married!

Seeing that kiss sealed the deal for me… This seven-year-old knew it was an actor's life for him! On the journey home, Hazel Malone, who we had not seen all day, walked down the coach and gave each one of us a ten-shilling note, (roughly 50p in new money). I was so proud of my first payday! I think of this moment now and wonder where Hazel had been all day? As there were twenty of us, she had splashed out the equivalent of £10 in payment. Surely, she was paid rather more than that to supply twenty kids for the film? I also bet she claimed a lot more for the cost of the coach and to have Sgt Major Gowans on active service. Over the years, and having been on her agency (spoilers!) I have my suspicions, though I do have to be grateful to Hazel, as she is the one who ultimately gave me my future. I still have that contract, which I signed over a one-penny stamp.

A KNOCK ON THE DOOR

I got home with the biggest smile on my face and showed Mum my wages. It wasn't long after my first starring role that I was asked to go filming again. Knowing how much I enjoyed my first experience, Mum and Dad couldn't refuse and before I knew it, I was off back to 'The House', as No. 26 Wellesley Road was now known to me, for another 6am call and a coach to our place of work. This time, it was for a film called *Edward, My Son*, starring Spencer Tracy and Deborah Kerr, who would receive a Best Actress nomination at the 1950 Academy Awards for her performance. The film was directed by George Cukor, the future Oscar-winning director of *My Fair Lady*. This time, I was to learn a whole new side of the filming process, as rather than filming in a studio, we would be shooting out on location. The setting was a school garden, where a parents' day was taking place.

I remember being called over to the assistant director, who explained that they wanted me to be in an 'establishing shot'. The huge camera and sound boom were loaded onto a trailer, which was to be towed through the school gates and into the grounds. I was told to wait for the camera to enter the grounds, where I would be waiting by the gate, and then run as fast as I could to the school building about 100 yards away. Well I did this once, thinking it was for a take, but it was in fact a rehearsal. Apparently, I did this well. I then thought no more about it and continued to be totally absorbed by all the filmmaking going on around me. After many, many minutes of setting up this sequence to go again, I didn't hear the call of "Action!" and as the trailer carrying the big camera was wheeled into the grounds, I was wandering around in dreamland. No doubt, Spencer Tracy and Deborah Kerr were wondering what had happened to spoil this take. The chaperone was called (thankfully not Mrs Gowans) and I was told that my important role was to be given to another boy... I missed my big moment and a huge lesson was learned.

George Cukor understandably never wanted to see me again. To add insult to injury, the cameraman on that trailer was the great Freddie Young, who went onto win three Oscars for his cinematography on *Ivanhoe*, *Lawrence of Arabia* and *Dr Zhivago*... I really knew how to impress! But this experience didn't put me off and I enjoyed many more days on set as a boy, being what was then known as an 'extra', though nowadays they prefer the term Supporting Artiste. I was on board the *Titanic* in Jean Negulesco's 1953 film; I ran through Sherwood Forest with Robin Hood, as played by Richard Greene; and I crossed paths with the likes of Diana Dors, Robert Helpmann, Alan Ladd, David Niven, Gregory Peck and many more on films that, I'm sad to say, I never kept details of.

I was just a little boy with a huge interest in what was going on around me and I really enjoyed being a very small part of it. During these early years of filmmaking, I asked Mum if I could have acting lessons at Corona on the weekends. I was, of course, influenced by the kids I was filming with, who were pupils at the school. Mum agreed, as I knew she would, and I went along to the school, which was situated just off Turnham Green. There I had my first lesson with Hazel Malone, whom I'm sure I paid more than the 10 shillings I got from my very first encounter with her. But by having these lessons, I was more and more inclined to believe that my future was to be an actor. Whilst I was enjoying every moment spent on a film set, the atmosphere at home was very different...

CHAPTER 3
Living At No. 7

I lived at 7 Burnaby Crescent for 19 years and have so many memories of living there; most are really good, some are moderate, then others are bloody awful! Burnaby Crescent was a road of twelve Victorian houses, all similar, fairly large with an adequate garden. All the houses were on one side of the road, while opposite were the fences of the back gardens from the houses on Burnaby Gardens. When we moved into the house, it was still lit by gas! I can remember it being changed to electric, but the gas taps in the hallway were to remain for many years. I liked the look of them and appreciated the way they evoked memories of the past.

I believe Dad's sister Joyce had something to do with us getting this house, which had four bedrooms and a scullery kitchen that was not big enough to swing the proverbial cat! Not being a house that he owned, my Dad saw no reason to do much to it. It was occasionally redecorated over the years, though Mum always hated what Dad did, as he would make all the decisions on colour, style and application! Dad had a very Victorian way of living, which applied to basically everything that Mum had to do around the house; the man worked and the wife maintained the home. They very rarely did things together, except playing the occasional game of bridge with people from Harrods. They would go just over the river to the Harrods

Depository in Barnes, where there was a club. I only went there once a year to watch their big fireworks display on Bonfire Night.

My first school was St Mary's, on the corner of Sutton Court Road in Chiswick. Apparently on my first day, I cried all the way there and smiled all the way back. I don't have many memories of the place, as I wasn't there for long, only one term. The school was later demolished to make way for the dual carriageway that would lead up to the M4. I don't claim that my attendance had anything to do with that.

My next school was Gunnersbury Preparatory in Burnaby Gardens, which was literally 100 yards away. I could hear the school bell ring and I would run down the road and was never late. Dad paid fees for me to be there, he always wanted me to have a good education and really worked hard for me to get it. I remember my first meeting with the headmaster, Mr Harold Pincott, which I found very daunting, as Dad needed me to impress and be on my best behaviour.

Gunnersbury Prep was a school where all boys were called by their surnames and you very rarely got to know anyone's first names. For me, being known by 'Dann' meant I had a lot of ribbing about being "Dan, Dan, the dirty old man, washed his face in a frying pan", which must have been sung at me a hundred times. It never bothered me though and I think my acceptance of the fun helped me to be popular.

In fact, any popularity I had was earned on my first day there when we went to lunch in the gym, which was on the first floor of the main house, accessed by taking the stairs on the outside. Along with other newcomers, I was put on a trestle table with the senior boys and prefects. The meal came and it was spaghetti. I had never had this before and the prefects told me that it was worms and that I had to eat it, otherwise it was the cane... None of the other new boys felt the need to impress, but for me the pressure was on to fit in. I took my first mouthful and said, "Worms taste all right." This was the best thing I could have done, they all laughed and I felt accepted.

I certainly enjoyed school for the first time at Gunnersbury, where we took part in plenty of sport. In the early days we played football and I scored many a goal. Another solid striker was a boy called Hudson, who I later got to know as Steven when he also became an actor in his teens. I'm not too sure how he got on in the profession, but it was good to know that we had something else in common apart from football.

The school really specialised in rugby and cricket and we used to travel on Wednesday and Friday afternoons to the Richmond athletic grounds for our sport lessons, as our own field back at Burnaby Gardens was not big enough for these events. We used to march about half a mile to Gunnersbury Station, catch the train to Richmond, then march another two hundred yards to the grounds, where we would change into our kit, but possibly only play for about an hour and a half, before we did the journey back to school. Extraordinary really. We also did the same thing for swimming lessons at the indoor baths in Richmond, which was a morning event. I remember getting my first certificate, a very ornate and fairly large one, for swimming a width! I felt so proud taking it home and showing my parents, I kept the thing for ages.

Mr Pincott was a headmaster who all boys respected. He didn't teach me, only the senior boys, but you were aware of his presence and I always saw him at the beginning of the day when we went across the road to church. Also associated with him of course was the fear of 'the cane'. I was sent up only once, for what I can't now remember. I wasn't alone waiting outside his door, as another boy was also in trouble. It seemed an age before I was called in, which was the first time I had been in his presence since my initial meeting at the school between him and my Dad. He was very pleasant and asked why I was there. I can't remember what I said, but he told me not to do it again and let me go without punishment. I also remember him announcing, on 6 February 1952, the death of King George VI. I'm afraid to say that internally we were all delighted about this, as it meant that we were sent home and had the rest of the day off school. What a disgraceful lack of respect, but boys will be boys...

My education at Gunnersbury faltered a little as I was often 'sick', because I was actually sneaking off to do quite a lot of extra work at the film studios. However, as far as the teachers were concerned, I was a very sick child, thanks to my Mum being very good at letter writing! In fact, I missed getting my polio injections as they were given at school when I was on a film set! Also, I didn't take my eleven-plus exams, as I was away working. When Dad found this out, there was a lot of shouting between my parents. I don't actually have any exam qualifications at all, which thankfully doesn't seem to have got in my way.

My first teacher was Mrs Pearce, who made me write right-handed, even though I was a total leftie. When Mum found out, she went down to the school and complained on my behalf, as I really couldn't do it. At the time it was compulsory at school for all kids to be right-handed! Thankfully Mum fought against this ridiculous rule and I was allowed to be a left-handed pupil. Amazingly my best subject was Latin, which somehow just clicked with me and I was often top of the class in that subject. The same could not be said for English however, as my teacher Mr Lowe was a total sadist. In his class, if any boy dared to speak out of turn or was not able to answer a question, out would come his ruler. You then had to place your hand palm down on the table and he would crack the side of the ruler down hard on your knuckles. I remember this nasty man with a lot of distaste, as he took great pleasure in inflicting this pain. Hence my knowledge of what a noun, precis, conjugation, adjective or any other 'itive' is could be written on the back of a postage stamp. I find it amazing that I became an actor, as it was only then that I began to really enjoy the language.

It would be good to know how the other boys at school got on in life. I am a fan of arranged parties and would love it if the boys of 1947 could meet up, have a pint or two and tell each other tales. Sadly, Gunnersbury Prep closed down sometime in the mid-sixties. Now the playing field and playground have become a small housing estate and the big building that contained the gym, classrooms and Mr Pincott's office and possibly his living quarter is now just a big house. It's strange when you return to have a look and realise how much the memories have faded.

Outside of school, I started to make friends who lived near Burnaby Crescent, including Barry Knight and Tony Wotton. Barry lived in Sutton Court Mansions, which we used to refer to as 'the posh flats' and I had to address his father as Flight Lieutenant Knight! Tony lived with his mother on the first floor of the house on the corner of the Crescent and Gardens. The three of us spent a lot of time together, mostly playing Subbuteo for hours on end, usually on our dining room floor. I say 'dining room', though it was only used as that at Christmas!

We were the first family on the street to have a car and as the road was our playground, Dad would have to move his car to the far end by No. 12, so we could play cricket using the lamppost outside our house as the stumps. The kids from Burnaby Gardens would also use our street to play in, as their street was used more often by passing and parked vehicles. So many games were played right outside my house. Also, at the end of the road was an area that had suffered a lot of damage during the Blitz, which we called 'the wreck'. In fact, the first V-1 bomb had landed about 200 yards from us in Staveley Road, which was a great place to play. We also had an anti-aircraft gun shelter we could play in. Kids today don't know what they are missing! I have many happy memories of 'my patch'.

Opposite No. 7 was the garden of the house in Burnaby Gardens that belonged to the Sayers. Two brothers, Norman and Anthony, lived there and were always playing with the rest of us on our street, which was very useful whenever our ball went in their garden. Once, the three of us decided to play 'Cowboys and Indians', but for some reason we decided to do this with no clothes on and we ran around the streets naked! I can't think why we did this, but we certainly didn't repeat it, as the result was the only time I ever got 'the slipper' from my father! Mr and Mrs Sayers then decided to emigrate to Australia, not as a result of my naked cowboy exploits, but because of the £10 immigration fee which was very popular at the time. I had to say goodbye to Norman and Anthony, though in the end they returned to England within two years, as Australia didn't work out for the family. Of course, their old house wasn't available to rent and the new occupants of their house started keeping our wayward cricket balls and footballs.

LIVING AT NO. 7

There were also now many more parked cars down our street, which made it difficult to play our test matches.

Eventually we lost contact… that was until many years later, when Anthony contacted me by phone. He was in hospital at RAF Northolt and asked me to visit. He had always been a bit on the ill side when we used to play during our childhoods, though now aged 23, he was lying in bed looking very weak. I thought he might never get up again. Anthony told me that Norman had moved back to Australia, while he had been serving in Saudi Arabia for a few years. Now he was back, he was going to leave and move to Bristol, where apparently he had a wife. I'm pleased to say that he did get better and I later received many an invite to go and visit him in Bristol, though sadly I never got around to it.

Over the years that followed, I often used to think back and wonder what had happened to Norman, Anthony, Tony, Barry and all the others from the Burnaby gang whose names I now can't remember. Life can be very strange however, and many years later, when I was looking for a cheap holiday I went into a travel agency in Hounslow and who should be running it but Barry Knight! I have no idea why I was in Hounslow, as I had never shopped there before, it was pure fluke. We swapped addresses and I later heard from him via Facebook that he was now living in Essex. With today's ease of tracking down old friends, maybe I will get to see some of the gang again?

Sometime during the late 1940s, it was arranged for us to have a live-in maid at 7 Burnaby Crescent, who was called Rita. I'm not sure why this happened, as the only thing I can think of was to have someone to look after me when my parents were out, though this as you now know was not a regular occurrence. Rita taught me how to say the alphabet backwards, a trick that I would then bore people with far too often. I can still do it, probably faster than you can say it forwards and I'm available for parties, weddings, funerals and bar mitzvahs. Rita was engaged to a soldier who had to go and fight in the Korean War in 1950, and for some reason to do with this Rita left, I never found out exactly why.

After Rita left, family life became fairly complicated when my Mum asked her sister Brenda to move in, with her husband, Len and their two children, Sheila and Geoffrey. They would use the two rooms at the back of the house, one being their kitchen and the other their bedroom. We all shared the bathroom and toilet. So all that was left upstairs was Mum and Dad's bedroom and a very small room for me overlooking the front door. I often wonder why Dad agreed to this, as the house suddenly became a little squashed. Mum said it was to be just for a little while, while they found a new place to rent. They contributed a little to the rent, though I hardly ever saw Len, who never came downstairs for a chat.

It was good company for me at the time as an only child, and Sheila and Geoffrey became my bestest friends. I remember writing a play that we performed in the garden, which must have been one or possibly two pages long, though I have no idea now what it was about. Sheila recalls that I was a very aggressive director… I suppose I was influenced by the work I was doing in films at the time. I was also an eight-year-old full of my own self-importance.

It was around this time that Mum became pregnant, which of course would present a problem with space at home. Dad asked Len and Brenda to find another place to live and it wasn't long before they left and bought a house in Ashford. Dad was furious about this and felt they had taken advantage of him

LIVING AT NO. 7

by being able to save for a mortgage when he had greater overheads. Dad and Len had never got on, which made it hard for my Mum and Brenda who enjoyed their time together. Dad told Len how he felt as they moved out, and when he asked for the keys, Len dropped them down a drain in the road. I don't believe they ever spoke again, though Mum would still go over to Ashford quite often to play bridge with Brenda. This was a game I was taught at an early age that became very useful later in life.

My baby brother Richard arrived on 21 January 1950. I can remember the thrill of seeing him for the first time and I was allowed to hold him. For the first time, I had a brother! Now that we had the house to ourselves again, I was moved to the rear bedroom that the Dawson family had used as their kitchen. This had to be altered and so once the sink and gas stove were removed, I at last had a big room of my own, while Richard was moved into my old bedroom with his cot and Mum was of course now confined to the house.

Mum then became a 'baby factory' as it didn't seem too long before she was expecting again. My brother John arrived thirteen months later, on 21 February 1951. I was now ten years old and had two brothers to play with at No. 7, which had grown into a house full of nappies. Then 17 months later, along came Ian, born in August 1952 on the, you guessed it, 21st! It was an extraordinary coincidence that all three brothers were born on the 21st, though I still wonder why it took them eight years to add to the Dann clan.

Mum named us all hoping that we wouldn't get our names shortened; I was Laurence though became Larry, Richard became Dick, John became Jaffa and Ian became Bub. All three of my brothers were very different characters; Richard was studious, John very cheeky and Ian the sportsman. Dad used to take us out to play football and cricket in Chiswick Park or down by the river at Dukes Meadows.

The cost of three new boys must have taken a toll on my Dad's earnings, but he was now a father who had got what he really wanted; four sons that he could be proud of! It sort of worked and Dad enjoyed his sons, though with respect Richard became his favourite, probably because he was really his first, as he didn't know me until I was about five years old. It didn't really bother me as nothing really changed in our relationship.

I was delighted to have my new brothers and the house was much livelier, especially when we got our first dog, an Alsatian called Josh. But it was a whole new world for my Mum having to bring up three young sons, with no washing machine and no more maid to help. She had a really hard time coping with her trebled workload and the sociable girl who had once loved to party and enjoy the occasional drink was now tied down for many years with the family. Dad was still set in his Victorian ways and continued to insist that she did all the cooking, washing and cleaning. I was told not to help Mum with the housework and not even allowed to do things like the washing up. I found it hard seeing her struggling to cope and so started getting more involved with taking the babies out in their prams or playing with them while she cleaned. Their marriage was by now very strained and it wasn't a happy home for me and I don't think for my brothers either. I decided to throw myself into trying to become a professional actor.

CHAPTER 4

I Did It My Way

When I was eleven years old, Dad had arranged for me to go to Wimbledon High School for an interview with the headmaster. I duly went for this interview, but afterwards I walked across Wimbledon Common with my Dad and we had a chat. I told him that I didn't want to go to this school, but instead I wanted to be an actor and go to Corona Academy. I have no idea why, but Dad said, "If you want this I won't stand in your way, but you will have to pay your own fees. I will give you a home and feed you, but I will not pay for your schooling fees if you go to Corona." I was very confused. What do I do now?

I remember having very little time to organise this, because if I didn't get it right, I would be going to Wimbledon, with Dad paying those fees. It was possibly the next day that I went to 'The House' and explained that I would like to come to their school, but my Dad had told me that I would have to pay my own way. I spoke to Hazel Malone, who assured me that there would be no problem with that, as they would get me enough work to cover my fees. I was ecstatic and couldn't believe what I had just heard. I got home and told Mum and Dad and to this day I still don't know how this happened, but my Dad agreed and I was given the green light. Amazing. My hunch is that Dad saw my passion for acting and gave me the impetus to fight for it. How lucky was I?

OH, WHAT A LOVELY MEMOIR

True to her word, Hazel did indeed get me plenty of work to cover my fees. I remember my first real part was in a film called *Made in Heaven*, shot at Pinewood, which was by now a very familiar workplace for me. I had a couple of lines in a scene shot on a big wheel at a fairground with another Corona boy called Vernon Morris, who I still see to this day. We were in this scene with the actress Athene Seyler, and as all the usual technical business went on, we ended up being stuck up in the air on this wheel for ages. I can remember Miss Seyler getting quite agitated about being left with two small boys 50 feet in the air, as I suspect that she probably had a fear of heights. I also seem to remember that us Corona boys had to do a Morris dance, skipping around a maypole with sticks that we were taught to bash against each other. I was paired with Vernon and by now we were obviously feeling like movie stars! These were fantastic times for me, especially as I was still supposed to be finishing my final term at Gunnersbury Prep.

Then in the summer of 1952, I finished school and joined Corona Academy of Stage Training. I knew the building in Sutton Lane in Chiswick, as I had taken private acting lessons there at weekends. It was a single storey Nissen hut with three long rooms, each probably 40 x 20 feet. The first room had large mirrors on three sides for ballet lessons with a piano at one end. The other two rooms were separated by a partition, which could be opened to make one long area. Just inside the entrance door were two much smaller rooms, which were probably about 15 x 15 feet. The room on the left was the girls' changing room, which had just a curtain as an entrance, and on the right-hand side was a smallish classroom. As with all the others, this room became studios in the afternoons for our acting, ballet, mime and tap classes. At the end of morning lessons, which focused on the usual 'three R's', we had to take our desks to the far room and pack them up out of the way. This 'studio' was then used in the afternoons for acting lessons, which was just as well as you could hardly move in it, let alone dance!

Outside were the toilets, one for girls and the other for the boys. The problem with the boys' one was we had to use it not only for the obvious but it also was our changing room. It was very small and extremely smelly as the urinals would overflow and you can imagine the rest. Of course, it was very cold in the winter and you didn't dare let any of your clothes fall to the ground. Health and Safety didn't exist in those days.

At this time, Corona Academy was one of only four stage schools. The others were Italia Conti, Ada Foster's and Arts International. Between them, they supplied all the young actors for film work. In my first term, I became aware of what hopefully lay in store for me, as at times the classrooms were fairly empty, with many of the older boys and girls off working in the exciting new medium of television at the BBC. The law at the time meant that under-12s were not allowed to appear on TV or in the theatre, even though I could work day and night at a film studio without receiving any education. Quite a few of the pupils quickly became very successful on television and you hardly ever saw them at school. I couldn't wait to become 12! I could take part in photo shoots for advertisements and I have a vague memory of doing one of these for a poster advertising knitting patterns! My brothers would later end up doing quite a few of these too, and as they were prettier than me, they made a lot more money than I did!

My first morning went fine; I was put in a class with the other eleven-year-olds and for the first time I was in a lesson with girls! The maths class was of the level I had studied about three years previously at Gunnersbury Prep, and I seem to recall we were reciting our multiplication tables only up to about the five times table. In fact, all my classes were of a very low standard compared to what I had been accustomed to. At the end of term exams, I got 100% in all subjects, so the following term I was put up three classes with the thirteen-year olds, and not long after that I was in the top class with the fifteen-year-olds. This didn't bother me, but frankly I don't think my father approved of this standard of teaching. I can't actually remember any of the morning teachers' names, as all my thoughts centred around afternoon drama studies. I think most of us were at the school for those classes, I certainly was!

My first afternoon class was to be ballet. All new pupils were brought forward and given the clothes we were to wear. I say 'given', but all our gear went on the end of term bill! The outfit for the boys consisted of a green t-shirt with matching green 'budgie smuggler' trunks that were knitted in wool and, at this time, came without a jockstrap, which left very little to the imagination. This moment became a real trauma for me, as I went to the toilet area to change knowing I would have to reappear in this outfit in front of girls! I acted like I was the only new boy and it took an enormous amount of courage for me to go back in. When I did, the class had already started and there were all these girls in tight fitting leotards. I grew up at that moment and it didn't take long to get over my embarrassment, thanks to this wonderful sight. I had now discovered girls and never saw them in the same light again!

I can't now remember the logistics of how the classes were arranged, but there must have been at least 50 pupils in that small area. I think there were four so-called classrooms for the morning and three in the afternoon. The one bonus for me was that I already knew a few of the pupils, as we had met during the filming I had been involved with during the previous four years. Then at the end of the day, we would all set up the desks and chairs ready for the next morning's classes. Despite all the natural trauma of going to a new school, I remember walking home with a feeling of having done the right thing. This is what I wanted and I had done it my way, aged 11!

There were so many things to learn, not just about being an actor, but my new routine at Corona. In the afternoon classes, we studied a different subject each day. I thoroughly enjoyed the mime classes, where we had a French tutor called Victor Azaria. He would conduct the whole lesson in French and the only thing I ever heard him say in English was "Take ze door" addressed to anyone who upset the class. He was a pupil of Jean-Louis Barrault, one of France's great mime artists. In fact, our principal Rona Knight had gone to Paris many years previously herself to study with him, hence the appointment of Mr Azaria. Sadly for me he didn't stay at Corona for long, but he certainly gave me the bug for the subject. In fact, later on I taught mime at many drama schools, including RADA and Central, which were known as 'Master Classes' (only because they were a one-off). I firmly believe that mime is an essential part of an actor's education, as it encourages a confidence in your physical approach to your work.

Another afternoon lesson was dedicated to tap dancing. Our teacher was Muriel Martin, who we addressed as 'Miss Muriel'. Muriel was the youngest sister of the Knight family and was married to a Canadian called John Martin, who also worked in the agency and had an amazing memory for phone numbers. It was always good to hear John's voice on the phone, as it meant that you had an audition or even that you had got a part. If you had to go up to town for an audition, you always went to 'The House' in Wellesley Road, where you would be met by a chaperone who would take you to Gunnersbury station, just a few yards away, for the journey.

Miss Muriel's tap classes were accompanied by two musicians, Rosie Cleeve and Mrs Heaphy. Rosie would arrive for classes as if she was off to a posh function, wearing flowing dresses with her silver hair beautifully set atop her face, which was always caked in make-up. Mrs Heaphy on the other hand was casually dour and always had a cigarette hanging from her mouth. She also never seemed to look at the piano keys, as her head was permanently turned to the class, watching our every move. Though as I recall, both pianists only seemed to know about half a dozen songs! Similarly, Miss Muriel only knew six tap routines to teach us. She would tuck her dress up into her knickers, so we could see her legs tapping away. But anyone with a modicum of talent could have easily learned these routines in one term, which made these the most boring classes. We soon realised that we were never going to learn how to really tap, especially as she would do these routines to the same tunes, which were so banal that I now can't remember any of them! I never understood Miss Muriel, especially as it must have been obvious that she lost the class on many occasions, but she never learned new routines.

Another afternoon was given to ballet, where we had various teachers until Isobel Florence arrived, who was a true disciplinarian, but with purpose. I thought she was a fine teacher, if you worked hard you got a lot from her. I never thought that I would enjoy ballet, but I did, even though I never really got any good at it. Although she once told me I did a 'double tour'. I preferred the double work, naturally, because this meant dancing with a girl partner. This made me much stronger, as we had to perform various lifts. When I think back, I could lift Janice Fields, a girl in my class who wasn't a small person, above my head and drop her into a 'fish dive'. Apparently that's a popular move in ballet, though I never found a reason to use it later in life! Another afternoon was dedicated to modern dance lessons, where Mrs Cleve and Heaphy, aiming to turn us into West End musical dancers, showed off their amazing repertoire once again on the keyboard.

Naturally a lot of time was given to drama lessons, where we were encouraged to improvise situations, learn acting pieces and take exams. It wasn't until you became a student at the Academy that you got to perform in plays, though we had some interesting teachers. I got a lot from working professionals like Thane Bettany, Ken Gilbert, John Nettleton, and of course Rona Knight herself, who would become such a huge part of my life and career.

At the end of term in 1953, I went up to Earls Court for my first acting exam at the LAMDA theatre. This was my first time standing on a proper stage, with the lights on me and an invisible critic testing my skills; quite daunting when you are 11! I learned my two pieces, did my own make up and made sure I spoke up. Then I came off the stage to be told I'd passed! That first time was frightening, but the second time and every time after was a piece of cake!

As I started my second year at Corona, I turned 12 and the greatest joy of this was that I was now allowed to appear on television and work in the theatre; the best present ever! My first theatrical appearance was at the Royal Opera House in Covent Garden - incredible, but true. I think there were only a few performances of Alban Berg's opera, *Wozzeck*, where I was one of many children singing a version of 'Ring a ring of Roses' to Irene French, a great friend from Corona who had a very nice part in the opera. At the end of that little song I had to sing to her 'Your Mother's dead', heady stuff! The best part was during the rehearsals, I sat on the front row of the stalls watching the huge orchestra playing. This was a big 'first' for me, performing in that majestic theatre and hearing that amazing sound. Not a bad start!

My next theatrical moment was when I was cast to play the 'Little White Boy' in Alan Paton's *Cry, the Beloved Country*, adapted from his great book. At the age of 12, I obviously didn't appreciate this very strong piece about apartheid in South Africa. It was to be performed at the Church of St Martins in the Fields in Trafalgar Square, directed by Josephine Douglas. The run was for four weeks and we rehearsed for three. There was no pay for the cast and crew, but we would share any of the donations given at each performance.

I was to be in two scenes, one with Neville Browne who was playing the 'Little Black Boy', followed by another scene with Neville and the great South African actor, Orlando Martins, in which he was trying to teach me Zulu. The production was very successful and played to full houses, which is perhaps a strange thing to say about a church? My mother chaperoned me and I think she enjoyed the occasion as much as me. When the run finished, I was given an envelope with my earnings, which were much more than I would have got from having a standard contract! We had a goodbye party and I met the young Australian illustrator who had created our poster… his name was Rolf Harris. Whilst I am glad I didn't keep in touch with him, I do still have my original copy of the poster!

I DID IT MY WAY

Our chaperone from Corona accompanying us to these theatre gigs was a gentleman called Derek, who us boys liked because he would let us play cards in the dressing room, which helped while away the many hours we used to spend waiting to go on set. Any other chaperone would not let us get away with gambling, even though we were only playing for pennies. That was until Derek started joining in… My Nan liked a bet on the horses and would often send me across the road to Betty Weldon's, a new betting shop on the high street that had just opened, to place her bet. It was she who told me that she thought Derek was secretly a bookmaker.

On one occasion at Pinewood Studios when a few of us were not being used on set much, we set up a card school in the dressing room. I remember Roy Hines, Alan Coleshill and a couple of others playing 'three card brag' for pennies. Derek was our chaperone and he asked if he could join in. We couldn't refuse, so off we went with the game. It wasn't long before he said, "Lets up the ante!" Very soon we were playing for shillings and the occasional half a crown. Derek was losing heavily to us, but he said he couldn't cough up because he didn't have any cash on him! He said that he would pay us later when we were back at school. I still remember that he owed me £17.10s and Roy was owed over £25!

We still hadn't seen any money from him, so Alan, Roy and I decided to go to 'The House' and confront him for our winnings. But when Rona heard about this, we were heavily told off for gambling and told that we wouldn't get a penny of the money! Walking away rather defeated, it was then that we all thought about this event more carefully and realised that Derek had only said that he didn't have any money when the stakes were raised; up until then he had been pocketing our pennies and thrupenny bits! We had been conned. A big lesson learned; don't gamble, kids!

I was also learning a lot about the medium of television, now that I was old enough to appear on the box! I remember my first experience was in 1953 at the BBC's Lime Grove studios in Shepherd's Bush, working on a musical show featuring a BBC orchestra conducted by Gerald Bright, better known as Geraldo, a very popular bandleader at the time. There were many guest singers, one of whom sang 'Papa Piccolina from Sunny Italy', to about six of us from Corona, no doubt chaperoned by Gladys. The scene was set in Italy and I sat next to a well, with my back to the cameras. In those days shows went out live and it was many years before recording programmes from home was an option, so I never saw this performance. I hope my back did me proud!

In fact, recording technology was so primitive in those days that when I got my first speaking part in a play called *The Teddy Bear* later in 1953, my memory is that it went out live on a Tuesday night and for the repeat on the Sunday, we had to come back and do it again live! The BBC didn't then have the facility to telerecord a programme and even when they did, it came at a considerable cost. In 1960, each 2-inch quad machine would cost the BBC £30,000! When you consider that this was 10 times more expensive than the average house, it was a lot cheaper to just get all the actors back in for a repeat performance. I have many memories of doing live plays and remember the sheer panic of having to change costume as I was running towards the next scene. This was equally a challenge for the technicians, who also had to move the cameras and sound equipment around the studio at speed in total silence,

I DID IT MY WAY

whilst the riggers rearranged the large cables to reconnect them to another plug area.

In one television play, I had a dormitory scene with David Hemmings, where, whilst speaking dialogue, I had to get into bed. Unbeknownst to me, the Props boys had made an 'apple-pie bed', which meant the top sheet had been doubled back so that I couldn't get my legs down to the bottom of the bed... this was going out live! I don't believe the director noticed what had happened, as I heard nothing from him afterwards, though I expect the Props boys enjoyed my scrunched up performance! Also doing some extra work on that production, which I believe was called *Big Time*, was a young man called Maurice Micklewhite - whatever happened to him?

I seemed to work with David Hemmings quite a lot over the next few years, perhaps most memorably on the big screen when we were cast in the film *West 11*. I remember our audition, when we had to go to the studio to meet the young first-time director Michael Winner... We were taken to the set, where Mr Winner was sitting in his director's chair. He hardly looked at us and instead spoke only to his assistant, simply asking, "Are they any good?" The reply came that we were and that was that. Later on, we had a day's filming on a street somewhere in Notting Hill, where we shot a scene with Findlay Currie. I had my Mum's car with me and so I offered David a lift back to the West End. That was the last time I saw him and he very soon got the leading part in *Blow Up* and went on to have a very successful film career.

Back to the small screen and my first big part in television came when I was 15, when I did two episodes of a very popular programme called *Probation Officer*, which was the first ever one-hour drama to air on ITV! It starred John Paul and David Davies as two officers who were dealing with kids in a juvenile court, and I was playing the problem boy in a story to be told over two weeks, which was a first for the series. What also made this job special for me was that it was the first time I ever got any fan mail and I can tell you I was glowing! The first episode was directed by Christopher Morahan, a very young director with whom I was to work several times.

My memories of live television culminate with an early episode of *Z Cars*, which was one of the last BBC series to go out live. I was in the tenth ever episode of this brand new cop show based in Liverpool, where once again I was playing an unruly yob. This time I was in a gang led by Tony Booth, who perhaps became most famous later in life as father-in-law to Prime Minister Tony Blair! To make live TV a little easier, there were usually some pre-filmed inserts played in, to give time for any costume changes or for cameras to repositioned in the studio. For this episode of *Z Cars*, called *Threats and Menaces*, we had a scene where I was the getaway driver and we were being chased by the cops, played by James Ellis and Jeremy Kemp, pursuing us in one of the famous Ford Zephyrs. At the finale of the chase, I turned the car over and was killed. I say *I* turned it, but of course it was a stunt driver, with dummies for the rest of the lads. It was great to watch the filming of this stunt, which he did in one take only. I remember that director Eric Hills was a bit naughty, as he did a shot of my hands driving, but got two of us to hold the steering wheel as he wanted it to look like I had two left hands… I wonder if anyone noticed?

CHAPTER 5

Coming Of Age

Turning 16 meant that I could work on stage without a chaperone for the first time. And I didn't have long to wait, as my moment came in 1957 when I went to Colchester to appear in a play by William Douglas Home titled *Master of Arts*. This was also my introduction to weekly Rep, and what an eye opener it was! We had one week's rehearsals, and I had no idea until I turned up that most of the cast would then be appearing in Noël Coward's *South Sea Bubble* at night! On Monday morning we had our first reading sitting in the stalls, whilst the set for *South Sea Bubble* was being erected on stage. Our director, who had the wonderful name of Wallace Evennett, gave us a little talk about how our set would look, obviously made up from previous productions. We then sorted out costumes and I was given the afternoon off, while the others got themselves ready to perform Noël Coward! I didn't know how these actors with major parts in both productions would be able to juggle two plays in their head.

I spent my afternoon off learning my lines and there were plenty of them. *Master of Arts* is a farce in three acts using the same set, the study of Ronald Knight M.A. I was playing Charles, Earl of Whitrig, who was found out to be having an affair with the matron. On the Tuesday morning, we went on stage using the *South Sea Bubble* set to stage Act 1. Then in the afternoon we plotted Act 2. I then knew that on Wednesday morning, before running Act 3, we would run Act 1 without books... I had to learn the thing in two days! Come Thursday, we ran Acts 2 and 3 without books in the morning and then in the afternoon the rest of the cast had to perform a matinee of *South Sea Bubble*! It was an unbelievable schedule, how did the actors do it? Well basically, they didn't... not very well anyway! On Friday we ran our play through twice, received some more notes and got ready for our final go at the play on Saturday morning. I then had the rest of the day off, while the other poor sods had two final goes at *South Sea Bubble* ... maybe they knew the words by then?

An abiding memory I have of *Master of Arts* is working with the actor Frank Woodfield, who was then in his mid-fifties, though he looked older. Frank never looked at the script, not once. When Wallace Evennett asked him why, Frank replied that he had played the same part, the Rev. Hildebrand Williams, a few years earlier and still remembered it... I can tell you now that he never gave me the same cue twice! Fortunately, I had the ability to improvise with him, thanks to doing a lot of this kind of work at Corona. Then while we were performing *Master of Arts* in the evenings, the rest of the cast were rehearsing *Hamlet* for the next production... frightening!

I remember I was paid £4.50 for the week's rehearsal and £5.00 for the playing week. A big problem for the actors was that you got paid by cheque on Friday after lunch, but in those days, banks would close at 3pm, so it was a rush to get it cashed for the weekend. These local theatres really relied on two performances on a Saturday to make the money for our wages! I got no expenses and had to pay for a return train fare from London, plus my digs at £2.50 a week and all my food out of this money. Amazingly I still had enough left over at the end of the week to spend £1.50 on a mantle clock for my parents, who came to see the last performance. I remember afterwards that Wallace came to say goodbye outside the theatre, but he was already so drunk that he walked into one of the pillars! Dad gave me a ride home and he told me that when he came backstage to see me, he saw the delight in my face sitting at the mirror taking off my make up. That was when he knew that I had done the right thing in choosing acting as my career and he told me he was happy for me. The other thing I can now confess is that I wasn't 16 until the last night on 4 May... I broke the law! Thank you Hazel for lying about my age.

Hazel had now set up a new office for her agency in Mayfair, perhaps paid for out of all the interest she was earning from all her 10% commissions, which she held in her bank account against every Corona student's school fees... Thinking back, she must have earned a substantial amount of interest from all the children's combined earnings before anything ever went to Corona. The Academy itself had also moved to larger premises at 16 Ravenscourt Park, near Hammersmith. We now had much more room for classes and the school started to take on many more pupils and provide much better education. We now had a proper headmaster in the form of Mr Cunliffe, who encouraged his 'best' pupils to take their GCEs.

I was chosen with a girl called Wendy and we were put into a special class with about six of the 'brightest' pupils, hopefully to get the first O-Levels for the school. I took four subjects; Maths, English, English Literature and French. I did pass my mock Maths exam, but when it came to the real thing I failed miserably, while Wendy passed. My father was not pleased, but my basic excuse was that I had little time to learn as I was working on enough TV and films to halt my progress. But as far as I was concerned, the main thing was that I was earning enough to pay my way.

Another huge change that improved Corona by miles was that we had our own theatre built at Ravenscourt Park. We actually helped build the theatre with the handy man Mr Lloyd, known to us as 'Yokker Lloyd' because of his dreadful habit of filling his mouth with phlegm with that awful sound. I remember one time sitting astride the top of the brick wall fitting the girders for the theatre roof. Not sure how we were allowed to do this, but I really enjoyed being part of building the theatre, where we would now have our own place to perform plays and musicals. I think I was about 15 when we started building and 17 when it was ready to be used. We put on at least two plays a term, where we would not only act but do the lighting and build the scenery, all in our own time after school. For me this was a fantastic time of learning everything to do with theatre.

The theatre was to be opened by the Oscar-winning American actress Joan Crawford and a plaque was made with her name and date engraved, which was cemented in place by Mr Lloyd ready for the grand unveiling... Unfortunately, Miss Crawford couldn't make the day so the theatre was never 'christened'. From then on, Mr Lloyd was known as 'Joan', which he got very riled by, though it was easy to get him going and many boys used to do so. Thinking back, he was amazing to be able to build a theatre with the help of students and I don't remember any other tradesmen helping him.

Colchester Rep might have thought I'd been 16 whilst working on *Master of Arts*, but completing the run on my 16th birthday meant that I faced a new dilemma. It was time for me to leave the junior school and the three R's behind me and become a full-time student at Corona Academy. I desperately wanted to stay, but the problem was I really couldn't afford to continue paying the fees. It had come to the point where my parents said I needed to start covering my overheads, paying for clothes, food and a little rent to Mum. It was understandable now that there were four boys to raise, and I think we agreed ten shillings a week. I went to talk to Rona Knight and explained that sadly I had to leave Corona. Then this amazing woman said, "Don't worry, I want you to stay on and I will give you a grant." Fantastic!

Thanks to the expansion at Corona, we started to have new exciting classes like fencing lessons, where our teacher was Paddy Crean, stunt double and stand-in for Errol Flynn, a huge star in the 1940s and 1950s famous for his swashbuckling films, always featuring elaborate sword fights and a glamorous co-star to rescue! Flynn had something of a reputation with the ladies and we believed Paddy Crean did too! I really liked Paddy's classes, not only for learning how to use the sword, but to hear all the amazing stories from his life. We also had a judo teacher for a term, basically teaching us how to fall properly without causing pain or injury, as well as lessons from an acrobat called Jack Le White, who was in his mid-40s but looked much older. In his first class, he showed us how to balance three chairs precariously on top of a table and then do a handstand on top of that. Respect was gained. He also showed us how to do somersaults and back flips, which were useful little tricks to try and impress the girls with. A class that most of us enjoyed was stage fighting and a fellow student who particularly embraced this was Barry Halliday.

Barry joined Corona when he was 18 and he got so good at stage fighting that he became a fight director. Working under the name B.H. Barry, he soon established himself as one of the foremost fight directors in England, arranging fights for television dramas and on stage for the Royal Shakespeare Company and many West End plays. Feature films followed and it wasn't long before he went to the USA and made a name for himself on Broadway. Barry and I got on very well at Corona and became lifelong friends. When he was very busy, if a fight was needed that he couldn't arrange, he would ask me if I wanted the job. I remember arranging a fight for the famous police series *Dixon of Dock Green* starring Jack Warner. I was already familiar with the series, having worked on it as an actor, playing a naughty boy who PC Dixon gave a good telling off, and got him back on the right track. But on this episode filling in for Barry, I had to arrange a fight scene involving three different boys, who all gave a different account of the event. This meant I had to arrange the same fight in three different ways. Not easy, especially as the time given to rehearse was limited, but I think I got away with it. You'll read about more of my adventures with Barry later on in the book!

I stayed at Corona until I was 21. A long time, but thanks to Rona's incredible generosity, I never had to pay a penny and I saw no reason to leave, especially as I was also working. In return for my grant, Rona asked me to start covering the occasional class for her, teaching the juniors in acting or mime. I was only too happy to do this and it worked very well for me, particularly as I found that by taking a class, I needed to respond to questions, which helped me learn as well, perhaps even more than the students did.

Rona also asked me to direct the play *Wait Until Dark*, working with the junior students for two hours each afternoon. We had to have the play ready by the end of term and I remember asking the cast if they would like to stay on after school to do more work, remembering that most of them were 16 to 17, and they did. This production led to Rona asking me to direct many more plays at Corona, where again I learned so much during this time. Giving advice and thoughts about how I wanted the play to look put a different kind of pressure on me, which I found I enjoyed. It was a very creative time for me and I felt I made a good job of my directing. I have an awful lot to thank Rona Knight for; she was fantastic to me and I owe her everything. Rona was also responsible for many an actor who went on to have a great career, including Francesca Annis, Michele Dotrice, Frazer Hines, Patsy Kensit, Nicholas Lyndhurst, Richard O'Sullivan, Dennis Waterman, Ray Winstone and many more. I apologise for not naming them all, but you know who you are and I am sure you are as grateful as I am. Thank you Rona!

Of course not everyone made it in the business and over the years I was at Corona, there must have been a turnover of many hundreds of pupils. Some attended because they were permanent cases for expulsion from other schools. Then there were many who came because Mum and Dad wanted to have a famous child, though that very rarely worked out and these kids only lasted a term or two. I had the impression that this was the case for David Tilley, who I had grown up with as a member of the Burnaby gang. I think his parents had desires for David to become a classical pianist. Like me, David started getting extra work in films, though being rather shy I think he felt working behind the scenes would be a better fit for him. He got a job at

BBC TV Centre in the 1960s and worked there for three decades, eventually directing programmes like *Jackanory*.

During the summer breaks from Corona, if I wasn't working, I would go away on holiday with my family. We either went to my Mum's sister Jean's place in Chichester, or to Dad's sister Joyce's place in Mevagissey. That drive to Cornwall used to be the biggest adventure, because it would take us two days to get there! I think it was a 350 mile journey each way and Dad's old shooting brake car needed to stop every so often to cool down! We used to camp with a small tent overnight at the side of the A30 somewhere in Devon, listening to the sound of sheep bleating all night. In the morning, after breakfast courtesy of our Primus stove and kettle, we would then head off again, armed with Mum's pre-made sandwiches for the rest of the journey. I remember we all had to get out of the car when it came to going uphill over Exmoor, as the car couldn't manage the ascent with the weight of us all in it. Sometimes the four of us would have to get out and I had to help push the car forwards! But honestly, they were fun holidays.

Away from the summer fun, back at No. 7 Mum and Dad's relationship had started to fall apart. It had never been great as far as I could see. Dad had got the sons that he wanted, while Mum had lost most of her joie de vivre. Money had got tight around the time I was 14, at which point we started to take in pupils from Corona, who would stay for a term. A little cash to help, but this was more work for Mum, and Dad still insisted that us boys should not help her with any of the chores. Things were now getting unpleasant. The day was saved for me when Maurice Lane came to live with us. Maurice was from Yorkshire and began his life in showbiz at the age of nine, touring in variety with his father, popular comedian Sandy

COMING OF AGE

Lane. He now wanted to learn drama and dancing and all the things that Corona had to offer. Maurice shared my room and being a little older than me, it felt like having an older brother. Maurice soon became head prefect at Corona and, being very popular, he would be invited to lots of parties and he would take me with him.

I was grateful for Maurice's friendship, as home life was now almost impossible and had got to the point where Mum and Dad were not talking. Eventually, Maurice decided to move out, not because of the atmosphere, but he was 17 and decided a change would be good for him. I was left behind, now without my good mate and facing this awful advert for a marriage. A better advert are Maurice and Sandy Lane, who as I write this have just celebrated their 62nd wedding anniversary, well done you two! I was honoured to be best man on their special day, which was done on a shoestring, as they didn't have two pennies to rub together.

Their wedding was booked for 3pm and Maurice and I had planned to get the little hall they had hired for their reception ready beforehand, arranging the chairs and tables, flowers, food and drink etc. I put on my hired suit and it must have been around 1.30pm when I went to the hall, but Maurice was nowhere to be found... I started to panic! I went round to No. 7 to see if he was there, as my Mum was doing the catering. Not a sign. Back to the hall, still no sign. There was now only an hour to go before kick off! The only thing I could think of was to go to Sandy's parents' house, where she was getting ready. I knocked on the door and asked the fatal question, "Have you seen Maurice?" I soon learned rule number one in the guide to being best man... don't upset the bride. I caused a certain amount of panic in the house full of mums, aunties, bridesmaids and children. I'm not sure which words exactly were uttered to me, but they made me leave in rather a hurry to further my search. I went back to the hall and, thank heavens, there was Maurice. He had just remembered that he hadn't collected their wedding cake. How much easier life would have been with mobile phones. We just made it to the church on Turnham Green minutes before 'Here Comes The Bride'. The pair of lovebirds were wed and I was forgiven.

But back to No. 7, where I was keen to avoid the awful atmosphere at home as much as possible. An opportunity came in the summer of 1958, when I got an audition for a production made up of two one-act plays, which was to tour Barnstaple and Exeter in Devon. I was being auditioned for the play *Purgatory* by W B Yeats, which was to be directed by John Dexter, who at the time I hadn't heard of, though very soon he would become one of the best in the industry. I was to meet John at the Royal Court Theatre in Sloane Square, a venue I had never been to before, but it had a reputation for the start of the 'Angry Young Men' group of playwrights, headed by John Osborne, whose play *Look Back in Anger* was playing at the time.

Arriving at the stage door, I was sent to an office backstage where I met Mr Dexter, who told me he was seeing me for an understudy part and to be the assistant stage manager. Slightly disappointing, but at least I would be working for a very important company. He then said that I would get the part as long as the costume fitted. Although I was only 17 years old, I thought I was fully conversant with the way of the world... I followed John below stage, to a storage area for keeping props and bits of costume. He then produced a pair of sailor's trousers and asked me to put them on. This pair had a flap at the front! They fitted and so naturally I thought that was it, I would be given the job... No chance! He then said that he could see my underpants behind the flap and asked me to take them off. By now the alarm bells were ringing. I explained that I neither needed nor wanted to do this and I left thinking that I would hear no more... But I got the job!

We went into rehearsals for *Purgatory* at a hall just across the square from the theatre. Graham James got the part that I had hoped to play, while the other character was played by John Phillips. My duties were to mark the floor plan and make copious cups of tea. I would have to buy the tea and milk out of my own pocket and then ask the actors for the money back! At the same time, the other play *How Can We Save Father* was rehearsing with a much larger cast. Somehow, I ended up being the ASM for that production as well! John Phillips was also in this play, co-starring John Moffatt and Robert Stephens, directed by John Wood. I was really enjoying my time working on the rehearsals for these plays, especially when I was asked to stay on at the Royal Court in the evenings and help out on *Look Back in Anger*. I was even asked to be prompt for a performance, though no one needed one, thank heavens!

During the rehearsal process, John Dexter had hardly said a word to me. I thought what had happened with my costume had passed and nothing more would be said. But then it was time to travel by train to Devon. All cast and crew were travelling in what was known as Third Class, while John Dexter was in First Class. Sometime during the journey, I was asked by the stage manager to go and see Mr Dexter in his compartment. I had no idea why, thinking perhaps that he wanted to talk to me about the part I was to understudy, as up until this point I hadn't had any rehearsal time. I got to the First Class carriage and walked along the corridor to find his compartment. The sliding door was closed, and the curtain drawn, so I knocked and he asked me to come in. He was sitting with a newspaper on his lap and told me to shut the door. Once I had done this, he lifted the paper to show me his erection. Unbelievable. Totally shocked I thought, "Oh no, not again". I think I said something stupid like, "You wanted to see me?" I can't remember his exact reply, but it was something along the lines of, "Do you like this?" I immediately left and went back to my seat, without saying a word to anyone.

We eventually arrived in Exeter and went to the hotel we were staying in for the week. We had a few days at the theatre to sort all the technical stuff before we opened. I think our preparations went well, as we had a very simple set and there were very few lighting cues. Whereas *How Can We Save Father* was more complicated, and I remember John Wood blowing his top when they were having problems.

After one rehearsal, back at the hotel I got another call to go to Mr Dexter's room. I'm not too sure if anyone knew what he was up to, but like a fool I went. Once again, I was invited into his room, where he was lying on the bed naked with a book resting on his erect penis. "Can you do this?" he asked. I left without a word and wondered what to do. I thought about telling the stage manager, but as she was a woman I didn't feel this was appropriate. So the next day, I spoke to Robert Stephens, who was the youngest member of the other cast and told him what had been happening to me. To his great credit, Robert went up to Dexter's room and I have no idea what he said, but I never had another problem. Fortunately, we were only at Exeter for a week, followed by another in Barnstaple. I never got a rehearsal, though thankfully Graham James was never off. Sadly I never worked at the Royal Court again, even though I had many an audition there.

Back at No. 7, Dad had now bought the house for a very good price, as he had lived there for enough years to be able to get the deal that the government had passed. And now that my brothers were old enough to start looking after themselves more, Mum decided to start her own business, beginning with a company called 'Hairdressers Bureau', the idea being that ladies' hairdressers needing trained staff could use the Bureau. Having been in the game herself, Mum was aware how difficult it was to find the right staff. She was very entrepreneurial and considering there were so few employment agencies at this time, she was way ahead of the game. The business really took off, but the problem was she used our home telephone number on her advertising, which made Dad furious. Every ten minutes the phone would ring, and we would answer saying "Hairdressers Bureau" and not the usual "Chiswick 1234." Dad made Mum close the Bureau down! Why they didn't just get another phone I will never know.

She then spotted that there was an empty shop around the corner, and suggested, "Why don't we buy it and get some washing machines for people to use?" She knew the problem of washing clothes at home and drying them without a machine, which were really expensive to buy. Dad pooh-poohed this idea saying it would never work and that we didn't have the money to invest. There were no other launderettes at this time; she would have been the first. Instead she decided to open a takeaway burger bar at Chiswick Station that did very well.

But being in a loveless marriage, she started to have an affair. We only found out when the five of us returned from kicking a ball around at Dukes Meadows to find the front door locked and we couldn't get in. Dad knocked on the door, but there was no answer. I climbed over the back gate, walked round to the back door and there was a man I recognised from the drinking club, The Riverside. He was the pianist. I'm sort of sorry to say that I confronted him and punched him in the face. He ran away, out through the gate and past the others down the road. It was sadly a classic case, with Dad finding Mum inside half-dressed. He told her to get out and leave. There were tears and pleas, but as you can imagine he was furious and he gave her fifteen minutes to go. The following day, she came to the front door and again pleaded with Dad to let her come home. I really don't know why she did this, but Dad said yes, but added even more restrictions on her, as if there could have been many more? I couldn't believe it could get any worse, but for Mum I suppose it did.

The dining room was turned into a room for Mum to live in and this situation lasted at least another five years, before Dad decided on a divorce and to sell the house. Goodbye No. 7, if those walls could talk... I think Dad got around £60,000 for it and I saw it advertised eight years later for £1.5 million! Well I know not how, but the judge decided that they should part by sharing the value of the sold house. Amazing! I was happy for Mum as this meant she could buy herself a little downstairs flat in Chiswick, while Dad moved to Leigh on Solent, quite close to where his sister Joyce lived in Gosport. He was really close to Joyce and became so much happier.

They should have done this years ago, but during all those years, Dad only seemed interested in making sure his four sons got the best education he could afford. Sadly with me being the eldest, I was the only one who got a private education, while the other three weren't so lucky as by the time they were old enough, money was tight. And what did I do with my private education? Nothing. Much to Dad's disappointment, though he did eventually become a little proud of me when he saw me being successful on TV, and even more so when I was on stage. I think he thought that was proper acting.

In adult life, Richard went to a teacher training college in Warrington where he met his future wife, Liz. They married with me being best man, and moved to Devon when Liz got a teaching job there. Richard never got the same luck and so he helped the farmer of the house they were renting, eventually agreeing to invest with him just as the bottom fell out of the milk and beef markets. Sadly he lost quite a lot of money, and this led to a divorce after Liz found herself another teacher. I know this hit him hard and I don't think he has ever recovered from it. He stayed in Devon and lives in a cottage in the middle of a field. After being an estate agent, which he hated, he's now a contented gardener for many a local.

To me, John was the brightest and cleverest of us four brothers. He was very well read and possessed the ability to play those quiz machines in pubs and empty them of their money. He ended up being barred from playing them in many a hostelry. John could have been anything but he loved playing rock guitar and made a good career out of doing house clearances. Anything he found of value, he would take to an auction and at times make a killing, while the rest of the rubbish he would sell on his stall at Southall Market. I often went to help him, because at the end of the day he would have many a bed, cupboard, and chair to deliver around the area and needed an idiot to carry these things up high-rise buildings. He eventually gave this up to become a full time rock idol, which didn't really happen, but chasing the dream made him much happier. John and his lovely girlfriend Sian bought a super barge on the Grand Union Canal in Southall, which he furnished with some lovely furniture that he had collected during his market days.

Youngest brother Ian went on to train as a plumber and builder. He was a workaholic, only interested in trying to make as much money as he could so that he could retire by the time he was fifty. He would even work on Christmas Day, especially for businesses that needed work done out of hours. Ian was a pretty good footballer in his day and loved a pint and his mates. He also travelled a lot and went to Thailand more than once, where he loved the beaches and the sun… at least that's what he told me! On one trip, he met a Thai girl called Sai, who was married but her husband was hospitalised following a dreadful accident on a motorbike. Sadly, he died and Sai couldn't afford the cost of his medical bills. Having now retired from plumbing and being a gentleman, Ian paid the bills!

They started a relationship and Ian decided to pack up here in England, where he kept a house that he owned and rented it out to make sure he wasn't short of some cash. He took Sai to the village she came from, many miles from Bangkok near the Cambodian border. There he met Sai's sister and her kids and fell in love with the place. He bought some land from a local, apparently the size of a football pitch, and built them a house. I have never been, but I have seen photos and it is really lovely, in fact it's the only house in the village with real windows! Clever boy. They have a son called John (named after our brother) who sadly I haven't met yet, maybe one day?

CHAPTER 6

The Day That Changed My Life

It must have been sometime in August 1962 when I got a call from Hazel Malone, asking me to go to the Theatre Royal in Stratford. Not the famous theatre in Stratford on Avon, but the infamous one at Stratford, East London, home to one of the icons of British theatre, Joan Littlewood. I knew of her reputation and that her actors were instructed to use the Stanislavsky technique, a performance method where the actor immerses themselves into their character's situation in order to help create a more believable presence.

I couldn't see myself working this way, but sure enough I was being invited to audition for Joan's new musical. I had never visited Stratford East before, though I had seen her West End show *Fings Ain't What They Used To Be*, which I loved. I gathered my courage and took the Central Line to Stratford. The journey took well over an hour and I was questioning how much I really needed to spend at least two hours a day commuting...

Coming out of the station, I had no idea where the theatre was, as there was no obvious signage. I asked a local and was directed down a road of terraced houses, which led to the famous Angel Lane. I wandered down and there was the theatre, looking incongruous amongst the rows of two-up and two-down terraced properties. I looked for a stage door, but there didn't appear to be one, only one entrance at the front. I entered the foyer looking for any signs of life.

There was a tiny box office to the left, then a pair of glass doors leading to a long hall with a bench on the right-hand side, which was covered in a green material. The floor was beautifully tiled, a bit like an entrance to a Victorian mansion or an upmarket public convenience. The walls were painted green, over embossed paper. I wandered up the hall to a pair of doors, which led to the bar. There appeared to be no one about, so I sat on the bench and waited.

There I sat on my own for what felt like an age. My nerves started getting the better of me and I worried about meeting the legend that was Joan Littlewood! I thought about some of the stories I had heard about how she auditioned actors, where apparently she would ask you to do all sorts of strange improvisations, sing bizarre songs, heaven knows what! After ten minutes, I lost my bottle and left for Stratford station.

I was a bit pissed off with myself for wasting all that time and money getting there, but there seemed to be no urgency at the theatre and no one there to meet and greet the actors. I thought, "Sod it!" I got to the station and started the walk along the corridor that led to the steps up to the Central Line. Coming down was fellow Corona student Clive Marshall, who had just arrived. We stopped for a chat and he asked how I'd got on. I told him my story and explained that I didn't fancy it. He replied, "Well now that you're here, why don't you come and show me the way?" Thankfully I did. Thank you Clive!

We got there and straight away a giant of a man wearing

a loose-fitting grey suit came out of a side door. I soon learned that this was in fact the stage door. I was called on to the stage, which was only a couple of steps from the door. I stepped on to the stage itself and wow, it was a beautiful auditorium, with three levels and four boxes, two either side, with a grand chandelier hanging down in the centre. I was gobsmacked.

But where was the infamous Joan? I couldn't see her in the stalls or on any of the circles. There was a working light, helping you take in the whole panorama. It was then that the man in the suit introduced himself as Gerry Raffles. I had no idea who he was, but he explained what the musical was about and that he was going to be directing it. I think the fact that it wasn't going to be Joan directing relaxed me.

Gerry asked the usual, "What have you done?" and other bits of small talk to get me a lot calmer that I was at first. He then got me to improvise about the last person I had met, which of course was Clive. I have no idea what I did, but it made him laugh. This was a laugh I would get to know well. He asked me to sing any song I liked, though to this day I have no idea what I sang. After about ten minutes of having fun, he explained they would be starting rehearsals in a couple of weeks and asked me if I would like to be in it.

This was the first time I had been offered a job on the spot. I said, "Yes please" and left through the stage door. I wished Clive good luck and off I went to the station feeling on cloud nine. When I got home, I phoned Hazel and told her how it went. I can picture her now, sitting at her desk, phone in one hand, the other twisting her hair by the side, trying to make a curl. I saw a lot of this strange ritual over the years. No doubt she was already counting the 10%. I was being paid £15 per week, which to be honest was not too bad for a small theatre in

OH, WHAT A LOVELY MEMOIR

1962. I couldn't wait to start.

Gerry Raffles was, as I got to know, the production genius behind Joan Littlewood's creative one. They were an item, living together in Blackheath. Gerry did all of the practical stuff, sorting contracts and finding the finances to pay for literally everything to do with keeping the theatre open. Joan was the amazing creative artist, in whom he had all the faith in the world.

My contract arrived in the post and I got the information I was waiting for. I was to play Harry in the musical *What a Crazy World*, written by Alan Klein and opening on 30 October 1962. There was no script for me to read yet and in fact I didn't see one until the first rehearsal. For me, first rehearsals can be quite daunting, as it's possibly the most nervous time on a job, especially on a new production when you have no idea of what to expect. I got to the theatre on time, one of the things in my career that I always took great pride in. Never be late! Going through the stage door, I was ushered up some steps to the green room. There were a few people gathered, none of whom I had ever met before. I was of course hoping to see Clive, but sadly he wasn't cast in the musical. I hadn't waited for Clive after my audition to thank him or to see how he got on and I am sad to say I never saw him again, from that day to this. Clive, I owe you so much, thank you!

In the green room, I was offered a coffee, which I gladly accepted and I started to chat to everybody, giving them my name and hoping they would do the same. The stage manager then called us together and we sat on whatever we could find as Gerry started the procedure of introductions. Alan Klein was introduced, who was not the wizened playwright I had expected him to be. Alan was a young East End songwriter, his song

THE DAY THAT CHANGED MY LIFE

'What A Crazy World We're Living In' had been a fairly big hit. I liked him immediately. In the cast was Harry H Corbett, one of Joan's actors whose reputation preceded him. His Richard II was legendary. It wasn't known to the cast at this point that Harry would only be playing the first week, as he was contracted to the BBC to star in a new comedy series called *Steptoe and Son*... We were only told about this just before first night and from the second week another Joan Littlewood stalwart Glynn Edwards, later of *Minder* fame, took over with minimum rehearsal. So, *this* was theatre workshop?

My major memory of the first night was completely losing my voice! This had never happened to me before, perhaps I was suffering with first night nerves, even though I didn't feel nervous, in fact I was excited to go on. I was the first to walk on stage in the play, entering from stage left (close to the stage door) carrying a ladder with Brian Cronin at the back. There were minutes to go before curtain up when I realised nothing would come out of my mouth! Harry H. Corbett was standing beside me and I gestured that my voice had disappeared. He immediately walked out of the stage door, into the foyer passing incoming patrons, and returned with a large brandy. He told me to throw it down my throat and within seconds my voice was back. What a pro, and a gentleman to boot!

Other names in the company that went on to have successful careers in the business included Brian Murphy, Avis Bunnage, Cheryl Kennedy and a certain Tony Robinson, later of *Blackadder* fame and now of course Sir Tony, thanks in part to his extraordinary archaeological work. Where did I go wrong?! I remember the rehearsal period being a lot of fun, which I now realise is what Gerry wanted to bring on to the stage. We had the amazing Alfie Ralston as our MD, who was very precise and strict with us youngsters to ensure we got everything right.

The show featured a punch-up scene, which Gerry asked me to arrange as I had done quite a lot of this at Corona. One of the reviews stated that the fights were too violent, which is probably the best review I have ever had! I did the usual fight gag of a kick to the face, whilst the receiver was laying on the floor with their back to the audience, then kick his open palm as he put a polo mint in his mouth, which he then crunched and after the kick, turned and faced the audience and spat out his 'teeth'. This always got a good response! *What a Crazy World* was the most exciting time of my career to date and I couldn't wait to do the next performance. Sadly the production was only to run for six weeks, as the critics hated it and gave us a good mauling.

What a Crazy World might have been panned, but it didn't stop a film version being made, starring Joe Brown and Marty Wilde. Brian Cronin and I were asked to reprise our double act, while Avis Bunnage, Barry Bethel and Harry H Corbett also returned for this big screen adaptation. Alan Klein wrote a song for us called *Independence*, which was about our characters getting a job, where we were painting the railings of a church at the top of London's famous Denmark Street, home to all the music publishers. We filmed this on a Sunday morning, soon attracting a crowd who were especially excited by the presence of Joe Brown. My favourite memory of Joe was when we recorded the soundtrack at the Abbey Road studios. We were working with a huge orchestra, and after hearing them rehearse one of the numbers, Joe approached the conductor and said that he thought the third trumpet was out of tune. The musician tried his instrument and sure enough, he confirmed

THE DAY THAT CHANGED MY LIFE

that Joe was right. What an ear! I don't think Joe has had enough credit for what a fine musician he is.

The director was Michael Carreras, famous for his Hammer Horror films. Michael asked Alan Klein to play a part, which was his only film role until he added a second in 1979's *All the Fun of the Fair*, which by coincidence I was also in as well! We also worked together again years later at E15, when I directed a revival of *What A Crazy World*. Alan was a fine singer and became well known when he went on to tour as the lead vocalist of the New Vaudeville Band.

Our six-week run at Stratford East was respectable in comparison with a production the previous year... Having said that I didn't feel nervous on the first night of *What a Crazy World*, I was visibly shaking when I went to audition for a new play coming from America, which was to star Stella Adler. She and her brother Luther had created the Method School of Acting, based at the Actors Studio in New York. They taught, amongst many others, Marlon Brando! This was the early summer of 1961 and my first audition for a West End production, a big opportunity and perhaps my excitement caused my nerves.

Running the audition was Frank Corsaro, a well-known American theatre and opera director. He was looking for six young men to play the bellboys of a Caribbean hotel. Backstage there were many boys, most of whom I didn't know. I wasn't my usual chatty self, as my nerves would only allow me to concentrate on my objective, to try and get the job. We were put into small groups and then brought on stage. I had never been on a stage in the West End before and my first impression was the bright light shining in your face meant that you couldn't see who or what was sitting in the auditorium.

We were to announce our names and then asked to improvise a situation about being bellboys and coping with a problem given. I can't now remember what I did, but my nerves seemingly served me well as I made the invisible audience laugh. Frank Corsaro then came on stage to explain that he was very happy with what we had done and basically said, "We will let you know".

The next thing I heard was that I had got the job! Hazel Malone called me to tell me details; wage, when, where and well done. The play was called *Oh Dad, Poor Dad, Mamma's Hung You in the Closet and I'm Feeling So Sad*. It was written by Arthur Kopit, a three-time Pulitzer Prize winner. But having believed this was a West End production, we discovered that we were to open in Cambridge at the Arts Theatre and then after two weeks, transfer to the Lyric Hammersmith. At least I would be rehearsing in the West End, and our first meeting was held at the Criterion Theatre in a large room looking out upon Shaftesbury Avenue, with cast and crew arranged in a large circle of chairs.

Introductions were made and we were told about the ritual of rehearsal times and fittings. Our costumes were all to be original, made especially for the production rather than hired in, including all our shoes! Amazing, I couldn't believe they were going to spend so much. Also, in the cast was Andrew Ray, son of the brilliant comic Ted Ray. I was to be his understudy, as well as playing Bellboy 1. It was quite a well-known fact that if you understudied Andrew, you had a very good chance of 'getting on'. Andrew had quite a pronounced stutter that somehow disappeared completely when he was acting, which I still find extraordinary. Andrew's wife Susan Burnet was also in the cast, as was Lee Graham, who later became Leapy Lee, singer of the hit *Little Arrows*. And my biggest cast buddy was Gilbert Wynne, who I continued to see for years after the production, despite us living at opposite ends of the Piccadilly Line. When our star Stella Adler arrived, she did so wearing a large picture hat and sat down without introduction. We then began to read the play. I had the first line, so I was apprehensive of saying it well... That sums up how I thought in those days!

The play opens with the bellboys talking about the new arrival at the hotel, whilst bringing her luggage into the room, followed by more luggage and even more luggage! Then it came to the point where Miss Adler's character arrived. I was looking forward to seeing how this icon of American theatre would approach the part. Well, she put her script down on the floor, stood up and without once looking at it acted out the entire play on the spot, never moving and only sitting down when she was not to be on the stage. In fact, in the second half she had a twenty-minute monologue, with the actor Ferdy Mayne just listening in astonishment to her rant. We finished the read-through and Miss Adler left as she had arrived, and we bellboys didn't see her again until a few days later after we had been rehearsed in. I seem to remember us having a few days off from rehearsal as well, no doubt for Miss Adler to rehearse her part in privacy?

After the rehearsal period, we were off to Cambridge. We had to find 'digs' ourselves, choosing from a list provided by the company. It seemed best to rent for the week at one of the University's lodgings and chatting amongst ourselves at rehearsal, we six bellboys paired up and booked three dorms. I shared with a young actor called Steven Berkoff, not knowing then the huge star he was to become on stage and screen. As I came to understand very quickly, sharing with Steven showed me that I was a rather naïve young man. Steven told me that if there was a sock on the door handle outside our room, I was NOT to come in... I also remember sunbathing by the River Cam in an area for men only, most of whom were naked... I told you I was naïve!

On the first night at the Arts Theatre, a few minutes before curtain up, I was standing backstage waiting to go on when Miss Adler came and stood beside me. I don't believe we had ever spoken before, as she was a big star and, I felt, quite an unapproachable one. She looked at me and asked, "Who are you and what do you play?" My word, we had been rehearsing scenes together for four weeks and here I was standing in a bellboy's costume! No more was said and on we went. In fact that was the only time we ever spoke off stage, even though I always made a point of saying good evening to her before we went on every night, though she never replied. I was actually *very* naïve and should not have interfered with her preparations, as she was Method after all!

One week later we left for the Lyric Hammersmith... then two weeks later we were given our cards! A lot of money must have been lost on this production, not on my wages unfortunately, but on all those especially made costumes and shoes! This is the shortest run in a play I have had. It was obviously not of our times, but it did come back many years later to the Piccadilly Theatre, where it ran for many more weeks than we did. Apart from our pre-costume fittings, the whole thing was over and done with in four weeks. Steven Berkoff has never contacted me since, even though I never removed his sock!

Back to my six-week run with *What a Crazy World*, which I loved, the only downside being the hour-long journey each way from Chiswick to Stratford, especially at night. But this commute was to be extended as Brian Murphy, who was going to be directing the next play to be put on at Stratford East, *High Street China*, offered me a small part in it. Written by Robin Chapman and Richard Kane, the play is set in Northampton, a dodgy accent to try and do... So I decided I wouldn't try!

High Street China is basically about three lads trying to get away from the town. One is a fairly successful local boxer and I played one of his mates joining him on his journey. I wasn't going to play this part at first, but the actor originally cast had, for reasons unknown to me, left after a week's rehearsal and Brian asked me to take over. Once again luck was on my side! After the caning we had taken from the critics over *What a Crazy World*, we got fairly good notices for *High Street China*, including some kind words about my performance, which was the first time I ever saw my name in print.

It was during the run of *High Street China* that Gerry Raffles asked me to come up to his office. As you might expect, my first thought was "What have I done?" But in fact, he confided to me that Joan was coming back to the theatre to direct, many years since her last play there. I asked why he was sharing this secret with me? "She would like you to be in it." Amazing, especially as I had never met her and had only vaguely seen her walking across the balcony from her office at the top left, which you could see as you looked from the stage, to the far-right exit where the accounts office was. This was to become a familiar journey for me, as I would later take that route many times to get to my usual dressing room, No. 4 on that same far right side. I wonder how many other actors have been cast by Joan without having to audition for her? Naturally the next thing I wanted to know was which production I would be working with the legendary director on...

I owe Clive Marshall (left) so much. Thank you Clive *(Author's Collection)*

CHAPTER 7

Joan's Army

Oh, where to begin with this amazing experience? When I have spoken to other actors who were present at the start of rehearsals for *Oh, What A Lovely War*, each one has a different memory of events. My recollection is that I was sent a copy of the script and told I was to play Johnny Jones, the young soldier being sent to the front during World War I. I read it and discovered that I had the lead, appearing on almost every page. I couldn't believe it! Me, working with Joan Littlewood and having such an important part. We were also going to have a five-week rehearsal period, beginning in January 1963, meaning I could enjoy a break over Christmas knowing that I had this unbelievable job to look forward to!

Come the first day's rehearsal and my nerves were really on edge. I arrived at the theatre in plenty of time, having no idea who else would be in the play. Thankfully I saw Brian Murphy, Avis Bunnage, Barry Bethell and Brian Cronin, along with Alfie Ralston, the MD, all of whom had worked on *What A Crazy World*. I had an inkling that Barry and Brian might be in it and it was comforting to see them, but what was Alfie doing there, as this wasn't a musical? There were a lot of other people who I didn't know and I wondered if they were actors or part of the crew? I remember Joan said hello to me and we had a little chat, probably about nothing in particular, but this was my first contact with the great lady. We all sat in the green room and Joan introduced everyone around the room, though because I was so nervous, I didn't take in any of the names of the new faces. Joan then introduced the author of the play, Ted Allen, and we then started the read-through. Considering my nerves and how much I had to do, I was fairly pleased by how it was going. We came to the end of the first act and Joan said, "Let's take a break. See you back in ten."

Back we came and returned to our places. I was feeling much more confident of how I was doing. But that soon changed, when Joan suddenly stood up and said, with a certain amount of frustration, "This is a load of fucking crap, we can't do this. All of you go down to the stage with Alfie and learn a couple of songs". I admit at that moment, I had absolutely no idea what was going on; Ted Allen the writer was basically being ignored, while some of the other actors seemed happy about Joan's rant, while I was, to put it mildly, very confused. I thought I had done quite well, but now worried that it was my fault, would I still be in whatever play we would be doing?

I think Alfie took us through "Row, Row, Row", which would become the first number in the show. It wasn't long before we were all called back up to the green room. The author of *Oh, What Lovely War* was no longer to be seen. Joan explained that we would be doing our own version of the First World War... with half a song that I'd never heard of before stuck in my head, my mind was really fuddled; had the whole play been dumped? Was I still Johnny Jones? I had no idea what the hell was happening! I knew nothing about WWI, which was certainly not a subject we learned about at Corona! Richard Bowlder, our stage manager, then told us to go to lunch, "Back in an hour please".

JOAN'S ARMY

Brian, Barry and I went to our favourite café up by the station. I had my usual egg, beans and chips with a lovely cup of tea. The café was very cheap and the food possibly riddled with botulism. It also had a pinball table, which you could play on for 3p a time, meaning that we probably spent more money than we would have done at a nicer place! Back at rehearsals there was no sign of Joan. We were on stage learning WWI songs and doing a little choreography with Bob Stevenson on "Row, Row, Row". Then it was time for home, and my long journey on the Central line to Turnham Green, followed by the 55 bus, was that of a 21-year-old actor with no understanding of what had happened that day...

I was aware that Joan had an unusual way of working, but dismissing the author and leaving us rehearsing without a script? I clearly had lots to learn about the ways of Joan Littlewood, who was nicknamed by some as 'Joan Hell'. I was still living at home in Burnaby Crescent, where Mum was very interested in how my day went... I didn't tell her, because I didn't really know how to explain. I later heard that all Joan wanted from Ted Allen was his brilliant title. Whether or not that is true, it does seem the most plausible explanation.

The following morning, Joan told me to spend the rest of the week at Stratford Library in the mornings to read as much as I could about the war. Then in the afternoons, I was to be back on stage learning songs and dances. This whole experience was becoming a total blur to me, I had little idea of what scenes we were doing and what songs went with which scene. The only thing I did know was that I was no longer playing Johnny Jones.

We had six weeks' rehearsal to get the play together. One morning we had the infamous Sgt Major Brittan come to drill us in marching and rifle presentation. What a voice he had, and he took no prisoners. I assumed this was to make us look like real soldiers, but as I was to learn later, this was far from the idea. We worked for ages on a scene in the trenches, based on the famous fraternisation between the two sides on Christmas Day, when the Germans and Brits met in No Man's Land, exchanged what gifts they had and then had a game of football. We improvised many versions of the play and after each day, Joan would rewrite and type out pages overnight for us to work on the next day. She did this with every scene. I have no idea when she slept. We rehearsed into the early evening most days, well past the time we should have finished, but no one cared. I certainly didn't mind, as I was beginning, very slowly, to understand what she was about. I was also aware that we'd had a few cast changes, with some of the actors given their cards and not replaced. That kept you on your toes!

 I learned that we were all to be dressed as pierrots performing on the end of a pier in the 'Ever Popular War Game'. This meant we had many different hats to wear and lots of props to work with. We were all made responsible for our own props and we each had a box to keep them in. No one was allowed to touch or use another actor's props box, under the pain of death! Songs and scenes were learned, only to be discarded. We eventually got to the point where we were running a different arrangement of scenes daily from a newly typed list, never to be repeated in the same order again.

 It soon came time to perform the first dress rehearsal in front of an audience. I thought this went well, but not according to Joan... We were called up to the green room after the show and told to be back at the theatre at 10am the following morning for notes. Joan's notes were usually posted along the green room wall for all to read. They were colour coded to your name, which made it easier for you to find your own. I think mine were in green. She used so many colours that some had to be striped, say blue and yellow, with every other word against a different colour. How she did this and how long it must have taken, I'll never know. My great regret is that I didn't keep any of them. As usual with Joan, this feedback session after the dress rehearsal was very comprehensive and went on well into lunchtime. Then we were back to do numerous changes in time for that evening's performance. After the second performance in front of an audience, we were once again told to be back for 10am for more notes.

I think we had four dress shows before we were committed to our first performance in front of the press, an extremely important night for the theatre, and for Joan and Gerry Raffles, who never took Arts Council money and had personally invested a lot of money into this show. A failure would have been disastrous for them all. My overriding memory of the press night was checking my box for all my props and hats and finding a new list for the order of songs and scenes. I noticed that I had a message from Joan, "After Avis has sung 'Make a Man of Any One of You', put on a boater hat and carry a cane and march on prompt side, behind Brian M..." What?! This happened about an hour before curtain up!

I rushed down to the prop store under the stage and luckily found a boater and cane. I then went to find Brian Murphy, who may I say is one of our finest actors and the nicest man you could hope to meet. It was whilst watching Brian work with Avis on *What A Crazy World* that I began to understand how real acting worked, he just make it look easy. And remember, it was thanks to Brian that I was there having this incredible experience, because if he hadn't asked me to be in his production of *High Street China*, then I wouldn't have been around for Gerry Raffles to offer me *Oh, What A Lovely War*. I owe him so much. With time to curtain up drawing ever closer, I wondered if Brian knew what this note from Joan regarding boaters and canes was all about? I found him and he didn't know either... My mind was racing, what was this new scene that we hadn't rehearsed and were performing on our first night, in front of the press no less? Well I didn't have long to wait to find out, as Avis' song was 15 minutes into the first half. Amazingly, I felt fairly calm and totally trusting in what Joan had asked me to do. But then whilst standing behind Brian, I realised that Murray Melvin and Griffith Davies were also in this line-up, similarly wearing boaters and holding canes. What was happening? Surely we weren't going to perform an unrehearsed dance to an unknown number?

Avis finished and as always got a great round of applause. Murray then marched on stage, followed by Brian, then me, and finally Griff. I copied what Murray and Brian were doing in front of me. Murray stopped centre stage and we followed suit. Then on came Victor Spinetti, screaming absolute gibberish at us. I cottoned on that he was giving us the same kind of military drill that we'd been given by Sgt Major Brittan in rehearsals. I honestly hadn't a clue what he was saying, but Joan had finally got what she wanted; a group of novice soldiers being prepared to fight. The scene was an enormous success, especially for Victor, who was brilliant. It finished with Victor getting Griff into a violent state of arousal, so much so that he jumped off the stage and chased one of the programme girls around the auditorium.

JOAN'S ARMY

At the time you don't give too much thought as to how and why things happen, but later on I guessed that Griff must have known he had to chase the girl and Murray must have known where to stop on stage? Had Brian secretly received any special instructions? If he did, it's a secret he has now kept for over 60 years! For my part I like to think, and hope, that Joan had put trust in me to be able to cope as the vulnerable one in the line-up? I must have done that scene over 600 times, but it was never as good as that first time. As an actor you can't repeat a true and real moment, only because you try to act it! Still I loved doing that piece.

Needless to say with the genius of Joan Littlewood behind us, the show became an enormous success, receiving fantastic reviews. We ran for 12 weeks at E15, much longer than originally anticipated. After each performance, I would get back to Turnham Green after midnight and then walk about two miles to get home, as the 55 bus had finished by that time. In the morning I would leave home just after 8am to get back to Stratford. I was being paid £15.00 per week, which was not bad money for the time. I still had cash to spend after the commuting expenses, but no time to spend it. Every night when I got to the theatre, there were queues of people waiting for returns, these tickets were like gold dust. We then transferred to the Wyndham's Theatre, where we performed for a year and a half! I think we would have gone on even longer, but we offered the amazing opportunity to take the show to Paris as part of the Theatre of Nations, which we won!

I have a very strong memory of playing the Sarah Bernhardt Theatre in Paris, where during the interval of fifteen minutes the audience applauded all the way through. We were there for a week and this happened every time. Another extraordinary thing happened to a local E15 lad that Joan had brought with us to help with the stage management. I believe this was his first job and despite not speaking any French or knowing anything about the theatre we were playing, he was a charming lad. One evening after a performance, he was alone clearing up and sweeping the stage when he looked up and saw a woman dressed in old clothes walking across the dress circle. He had no idea who she was, but she was limping and he became frightened when she wouldn't respond to him. It is believed that he had in fact seen the ghost of Sarah Bernhardt, who it was claimed used to walk the circle and had a wooden leg, hence the limp he noticed. I now believe in ghosts!

After Paris we came back to Stratford to rehearse a production of *Henry VI: Parts One and Two*, which we were to perform at the Edinburgh Festival. Then after Edinburgh, we would be taking *Oh, What A Lovely War* to America and performing on Broadway, incredible! It was at this point that there were a number of cast changes; a couple were voluntary as I know that some of the cast didn't want to go to America, including Avis Bunnage, who was replaced by Barbara Windsor. Others sadly had no say, as one of the stipulations of entry into the American theatre was that we had to employ four US actors; two men and two women. American Equity is very powerful. I was already feeling like the luckiest person to be a small cog in this theatrical masterpiece, but to now have the opportunity to take the show to America? Incredible! And what an adventure it was…

CHAPTER 8
Living in America

Before we played Broadway, we were to perform *Oh, What A Lovely War* at the Forrest Theatre in Philadelphia for four weeks, mainly to work in our newcomers; Marcia Rodd, Linda Loftis, Jack Eddleman and Reid Shelton, a highly experienced actor who went on to play the original Daddy Warbucks in *Annie*. As we were the youngest in the cast, I spent most of my downtime with Linda Loftis, a former Miss Texas, and we went to many jazz clubs after dark, which resulted in us making the gossip pages in the press! I was later invited to her wedding in Texas, but couldn't go as it would have been very expensive; thankfully I had the excuse that I was working.

I very much enjoy talking about jazz to anybody who will listen, and backstage at the Forrest Theatre was a lady working as one of the fly operators (then ironically labelled as a 'Flyman') responsible for pulling the scenery up and down using ropes, which at this theatre were stage level. Anyway, we got on to jazz and she told me that the legendary musician John Coltrane was playing that night and she gave me the address. After the show, I got a taxi to take me there, but when the driver dropped me off, I couldn't see any sign of a jazz club. It was 11pm and I was stood alone in a residential street of large terraced houses, probably six storeys high. Where's this club? I found the street number given to me and I walked up the stone stairs, but couldn't find any knocker, bell or even a sign. I banged with my fist, expecting no response, but suddenly a sliding panel at head height opened and I was greeted by a pair of eyes! "Yes?" they asked. In my best English voice I politely replied, "I believe John Coltrane is playing here tonight?" The panel closed, the door opened and I was invited in. I didn't have to pay anything and I was shown to a door, from behind which I could hear the sound of live music. I entered and it was Coltrane playing with a quintet, my first real experience of jazz life! I stayed until the end and had a fantastic night.

I had another 'first' experience whilst doing the sights as a tourist. I had just seen the Liberty Bell and then a short walk later I came across the City Hall, a huge Victorian building where the Mayor of Philadelphia works. I thought I'd explore inside and was happily wandering around upstairs, just looking with no one else around. I came to a large door and thought I'd see what was in there... I walked into this huge room to find a large desk at the far end, with a man sitting behind it. I was about to ask some inane question when out of nowhere, a uniformed security officer burst in, pointing a gun at me! It turned out I had walked into the mayor's office. I again adopted my best polite English accent and was escorted out of the building, fortunately without being arrested or fined. I think I must have given them some food for thought about their security arrangements, which I like to think of as my gift to the USA.

But it seemed that Joan felt that she had to give our American friends a gift in return and as a result, my role on the production was greatly diminished. When we started in Philadelphia, I was playing seventeen parts in the show, but by the time we got to Broadway, most of my parts were given to Jack and Reid and I was left with only four characters to play; the drill scene, the Irish jig dance, a newsboy and a plant pot in Buckingham Palace... I was 3,000 miles from home and feeling really low. I already knew that Joan was a prolific note giver, but despite me having already performed the show hundreds of times in England, she was giving me dozens of notes on the little I had left to do, none of them complimentary. We played our four weeks in Philly, once again to good reviews, then we were off to Broadway...

We had a week of rehearsals at the Broadhurst Theatre on 44th Street before our opening night and I couldn't have been lower, with Joan still giving me note upon note. About one hour before curtain up, I got a call over the Tannoy, "Can Larry Dann go to the stage door." I thought, "What now?" I left my shared 'dressing room' under the stage, which was actually a series of curtains draped together to offer some sort of privacy, arrived at the stage door and was greeted by my mother's brother, my Uncle Ian! He worked in Connecticut for Mobil Oil and was in New York on business and wanted to wish me good luck. He couldn't come to see the show, but it was great to see him and this unexpected surprise gave me a lift.

We said our goodbyes and I turned to go back inside and there was Joan. She called me to one side and said, "take all your parts back tonight, those Yankees are useless". WTF was going on?! I didn't tell anyone, not even Jack who had been given most of my stuff. I just felt so happy again. I did the show, and afterwards Joan came to see me and said, "That's better, that's what I want from you". She had felt I was getting too big for my boots, enjoying the success without working for it and had pulled me down to build me back up. That might sound rough, but I am so grateful to her for trusting me. Over the many years we worked together, Joan taught me to be humble.

Traditionally after a first night, there is a party whilst the company waits for the reviews to come in. Our party was at the top of a skyscraper on 5th Avenue, in a very posh reception area called the Rainbow Room. Before going there, Brian Murphy said he was going to Sardi's right opposite the Broadhurst and invited me to join him. Apparently, this was the place to be seen and it was packed. Walking through a sea of faces I didn't recognise, I suddenly noticed someone I knew all too well; John Dexter, the pervert director who had tried it on with me in Devon when I was only 17! I was on such a high from the performance that I just gave him a glare of recognition, said nothing and walked away. It was *my* night and he could get stuffed. We couldn't stay long at Sardi's as we were to be at the party by 11pm and I remember getting a cab to take us to the Rainbow Room.

Arriving very high up in this skyscraper, I walked into the party room, but there was hardly anyone there. Just a few waiting staff carrying some silver trays offering champagne, canapés and all sorts of little luxuries. I had never been to a reception of this magnitude before and whilst I was enjoying the food and drink, I couldn't help but wonder where all the other guests were? There was no one else there but the cast and crew. It was well after midnight when someone rushed into the room and screamed, "the reviews are great!" Suddenly the room filled with dozens of strangers, all full of praise and congratulating each of the cast. I was given to understand that if the crits had been bad, it would have been

LIVING IN AMERICA

the first plane home! Despite our success, strangely I don't think Joan or Gerry were there.

During that hectic first week of rehearsals in New York, a number of us had been put in a hotel on Times Square, which was convenient as it was very close to the Broadhurst. My room was very small and I shared it with a family of cockroaches, the first time I had met any of those creatures. I also learned that New York really is the city that never sleeps and with the hotel being on Times Square, it was incredibly noisy. The morning after our successful first night, I had a chat with Frank Coda, one of the actors who had joined the company at Edinburgh. Frank and his wife Debbie, who had travelled with him for the trip, agreed that the hotel was crap and we all decided that, as we now knew we would be staying a while, we would find somewhere else to stay at the first opportunity!

We searched the papers for any rooms we could let and we found a place on West 73rd Street called the Bristol Hotel. They were offering short lets, which of course was ideal. But when we got there, we discovered that it wasn't strictly what you would call a hotel, as there was no restaurant. Instead, all the rooms had a small kitchen so you could cook for yourselves. The only thing that really made it a hotel was that the rooms were cleaned every day, which was excellent! We asked the reception if there were any rooms to let and by luck there was a 'room' with two bedrooms, a kitchen, bathroom and living room, offered at a price that would work well for the three of us to share. So we did! With nice views towards Central Park, Frank, Debbie and I lived happily on the 12th floor for the rest of the run!

OH, WHAT A LOVELY MEMOIR

New York is arguably the greatest city in the world for jazz and I must have visited about twenty clubs to see my heroes perform live. I saw John Coltrane again, this time at Birdland Jazz Club, where, as it wasn't a full house, I got a table fairly close to the stage. When Coltrane finished his first set, the great Mose Allison came on; I didn't realise I would get a double whammy! Then Elvin Jones, Coltrane's drummer, came over to my table and asked if I had a pen? I did and lent it to him and watched as he scribbled something on a piece of paper. He then gave my pen back, mumbled some thanks and left me to glow alone. I'm such a groupie!

Something similar happened to me at another club, where I'd taken Linda Loftis to see the great bass player Charlie Mingus. Once again I was lucky to get a table next to the stage. After a number, Mingus picked up his bass and placed it on our table, where he got out a small hacksaw and sawed off the end of his peg, the piece that sticks out of the bottom of the bass to adjust the height. Off he went back on stage, without saying a word to us and started playing again. I picked up the peg, put it in my pocket and then placed it on the mantelpiece back at the hotel for show, what a bonus! Sadly whoever cleaned the room the next day threw it away thinking it was rubbish!

Speaking of which, New York City itself was dirty and suffered from a lot of crime. I was told not to use the subway home at night and take a cab instead. Being the old miser I am, I ignored the warnings and took the subway, where I often saw gangs walking the length of the train, no doubt looking for trouble. I used to just sit there looking at the ground as advised and thankfully was never bothered. In fact on my first day in NY, I wandered around Times Square and came across a man lying dead flat across the pavement, with people either walking around or stepping over his body! On another occasion, I was going to the Worlds Fair over in Brooklyn, a huge event where almost every country in the world had an area to show off their image. I took the subway early and it was fairly empty. Towards the end of the line where the event was being held, the doors wouldn't shut at one of the stations and the guard was continually trying to get them to close, but they only got so far before opening again. This went on for about a minute and then I noticed what the problem was; there was a man lying unconscious, blocking the doors. He was at the far end of the carriage and no one was taking any notice. So muggins here got up to investigate. I looked around for help, but no one would assist, as the doors continued to crash against him. I grabbed him under his arms and lifted him off the train and onto the platform. Immediately the doors closed behind me and the train hurtled off, leaving me on a deserted platform high up over a road with not a soul to be seen, only this unconscious man for company. He was still breathing, so I decided to leave him and see if I could find someone who worked at this station.

I started to go down the stairs to the road below when a man in a railway uniform, who looked like a ticket inspector, was coming up towards me. I told him what had happened and asked him if he could call an ambulance. He refused and said that I would have to call it, because whoever did would have to pay for the ambulance and the man's treatment! I couldn't believe it and protested that this man was nothing to do with me and surely the station should be looking after ill passengers? Suddenly another train arrived and I made the snap decision to jump on and leave. I still feel bad about this all these years later and have often wondered what happened to that man.

Back on stage, the show was proving a huge success and the five of us in the drill scene were asked to do one of America's top variety TV shows, which was a marvellous opportunity. On the same bill was Kermit the Frog, making a very early television appearance many years before *The Muppet Show*. We were to perform this show on a Sunday and I would be paid my usual weekly fee, which would make some very useful extra cash. But there was a catch; we were told that we had to join the TV union for a one-off fee of $250, which - you guessed it - was my weekly wage! I think they saw us coming. I couldn't believe it, but I had no choice, as I couldn't let Joan or any of the other actors down. They also had to pay, but as they were on a larger wage than me they at least came away with some pocket money. Added to this was the fact that American Equity were taking 10% of my theatre wages and after the American tax man took his share as well, you can imagine that I didn't come home with much left!

I also learned that anything goes in America when just after New Year's Day 1965, we were told at the Wednesday Matinee that the play was coming off on Saturday night! What? Four days' notice! Apparently Gerry Raffles had a disagreement with the American producer David Merrick and that was that. I was shattered. I still had another five months left on my contract, but in America they only had to pay out an obligatory two weeks' wages! I don't recall how, when or where I got my plane ticket home, but I do remember being able to see Churchill's coffin lying in state at Parliament.

I had some good times in New York for which I am grateful, and I met some lovely people during my time there, including Arthur Renzulli, the bass player for *Hello Dolly* which was playing just across the road from us on 44th. Arthur took me, Frank and Debbie over to his parents' place out in the country for the day. There we met his father, who had played in goal for the USA when they beat England in a World Cup game. Arthur also introduced us to Mr Yashica, the owner of Yashica Cameras, who sold me a 35mm film camera very cheaply. We spent a lot of time with Arthur, mostly having a beer after the evening show or playing ten pin bowling in the Theatre League, against many well known stars. At one game, we played against *Golden Boy*, the Sammy Davis Jr. musical, where the great man himself paid for everyone's fees and food because he couldn't turn up. I'd rather have met him!

Though of course, what I was most grateful for at the end of this adventure was that I had met and worked with the genius Joan Littlewood. And I thanked my lucky stars when Joan once again invited me, via Gerry, to work with her on a play with music called *Forward Up Your End* written by Ken Hill. This was a very funny piece about Birmingham and its dodgy council, though the songs themselves were not the best. Gerry knew that I played a bit of piano and asked me if I would like to write a couple of songs. I jumped at the chance and, with Jenny Logan singing the words, I'm pleased to say one critic thought our song 'Don't Fly Away' was the best in the show. I believe this earned me another bonus point with Joan, who overall I worked with for 14 years, including on many new plays as well as Sunday cabarets, where she mostly made me Master of Ceremonies, a blooming awful job as most of the time you had no idea what would be happening next.

After this, Ken Hill took over as director of the theatre and I was given my first play to direct there, a new version of

OH, WHAT A LOVELY MEMOIR

What a Crazy World, where Alan Klein and I worked on a more modern version of East End youth. But during rehearsals, Gerry Raffles sadly died in France and from that day, Joan never wanted to set foot in the theatre again. This was particularly heartbreaking for me, as it meant that Joan would never see my work as a director. I basically owe Joan everything, she taught me not to act, but react. She regularly showed up at a theatre I was performing in, often to tell me that the play I was doing was crap, but that I was really good. Bless you Joan, I cannot express enough what I felt for you.

I returned from the US of A in some ways with much more than I went with. I had at least two more suitcases, one carrying a fairly large telescope that I had bought for my brothers, plus presents for my parents. I had also brought back copious copies of newspapers containing any reports about the play. But my finances were not as they should be. When I was contracted by Gerry Raffles, I knew I would receive the equivalent in dollars of £80 a week, which seeing as I was getting £25 in London was amazing, but by the time I'd paid for accommodation and food, I came back home with no profit. But never mind, I'd had a fantastic time over there and learned a great deal from Joan. At least I hadn't made a loss...

Then I got a real shock, a love letter from the British taxman containing a huge bill for 50% of my American earnings! Now I was in debt, owing over £1,000 that I simply didn't have. I had to get a job and fast. Thankfully Bob, the owner of Chiswick Minicabs, came to the rescue and gave me a job driving his cars. I drove for 12 hours a day and was allowed to keep half the takings, so I ended up doing very well out of this, thank you. After a few weeks, I got notice that the USA taxman was sending me back all the tax that I

LIVING IN AMERICA

had paid them, now that I had settled up all my British tax. The good news was that I got more back than I had paid in British tax and ended up with a few hundred quid to play with. Result!

I decided to keep my driving job, as Bob was great about letting me go off if I got an acting job and then drive for him again when I was ready. I've been very lucky throughout my life to have some brilliant people in my corner and he was one of them, thank you Bob. I also enjoyed the fact that I would pick up all sorts of people, which was a very useful exercise for an actor. I once got an early call to an address in Chelsea to take someone to Hounslow. When I arrived, it was obvious that the lady coming down the concrete steps to get into my cab was not of this parish and also slightly worse for wear. She barely said a word, even though she wanted to sit in the front. I took her to the address given and asked for the fare. She then said, "I have no cash, but I'll give you a blowjob?" I think I replied in my perfect English accent, "I'd prefer cash thank you and if not, I will take you to the nearest police station..." I got the cash.

During the 1966 World Cup, us cabbies would watch the telly while we were waiting in the office for our next fare, where it was a case of first come first served. I was next and being engrossed in the match, I didn't want the phone to ring, but it did. I was asked to pick up a man waiting at the Chiswick roundabout and take him to Heathrow Airport. I would find him waiting by the RAC box (remember them?) I left the office cursing my luck at missing the rest of a good game. I got to said RAC box and, lo and behold, there was a young man with a suitcase waiting. He got in my Cortina and I realised that he was Luis Suárez, the Spanish centre forward who had only just been knocked out of the competition the previous day. I tried to chat to him about the Cup, but he spoke very little English. He didn't tip me very much either! I got back to the office where no one would believe my story. I drove for Bob for about six months, after which I was ready to reach for the stars again, with many characters etched in my brain.

Revisiting the Broadhurst Theatre in New York, 2023. *(Author's Collection)*

(L-R) my grandmother Helen Forbes, my mother Barbara Forbes, my grandfather Christian Dann, my father Norman Dann, my grandmother Rosa Dann. *(Author's Collection)*

Posers! With my beautiful mother, Barbara, who enjoyed taking part in amateur drama. Sadly my father had more Victorian ideas for her. *(Author's Collection)*

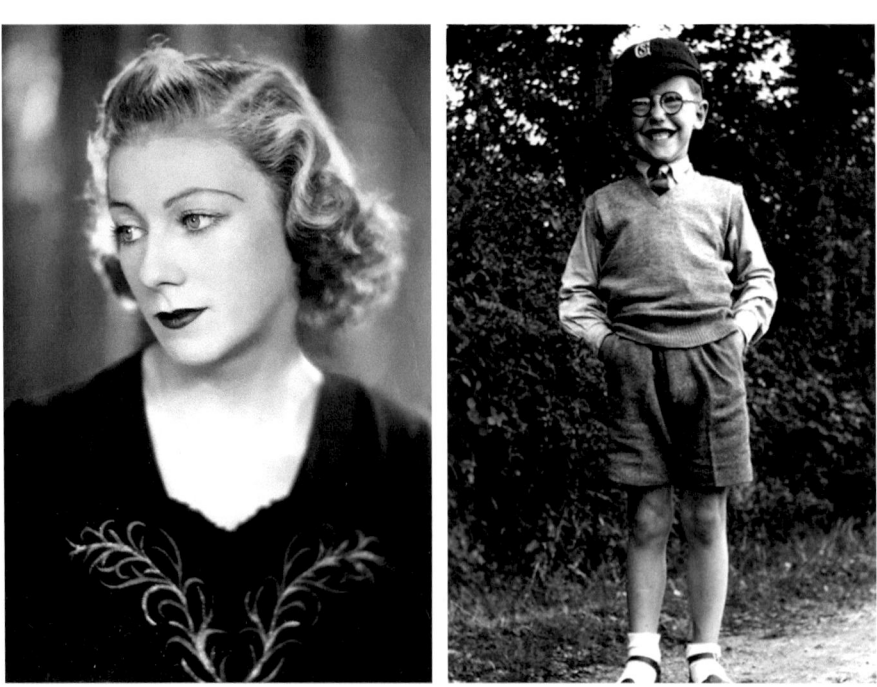

One of Mum's headshots. *(Author's Collection)* Off to be a film extra. *(Author's Collection)*

With Dad and my brothers John, Ian and Richard in the garden at No. 7.
(Author's Collection)

Above: One of my first headshots and an early theatre gig with Neville Browne in *Cry, the Beloved Country* in 1953. Below: Corona Days *(Author's Collection)*

Meet the band Method! (L-R) Paul Lynton, Stewart Guidotti, me, Jimmy Luck and John Sago. We weren't destined to become sex symbols. *(Author's Collection)*

Filming *Oh What A Crazy World* with Marty Wilde, Joe Brown and Brian Cronin. *(Author's Collection / Warner-Pathe Distribution)*

A rare day of filming for me on *Before Winter Comes* with David Niven, Topol and John Collin. I spent most of the eight-week shoot sightseeing in Austria *(Author's Collection)*

On top of the world! Enjoying a spot of sunbathing on a mountain with Colin Spaull during the making of *Before Winter Comes* in Anif, April 1968. *(Author's Collection)*

Left: Colin and I on set with David Niven. Right: Another day off! *(Author's Collection)*

Rehearsing a political piece at the Palladium with Brian Murphy, Vanessa Redgrave and Murray Melvin. *(Author's Collection)*

Filming *Ghost Story* in India with Vivian MacKerrell and Murray Melvin.
(Ghost Story is available on Blu-ray from Nucleus Films)

Poor old Talbot didn't have a comfortable stay in the haunted mansion.
(Ghost Story is available on Blu-ray from Nucleus Films)

Avoiding eye contact with the very funny Kenneth Connor on *Carry On England*, alongside Windsor Davies and Tricia Newby. *(Author's Collection)*

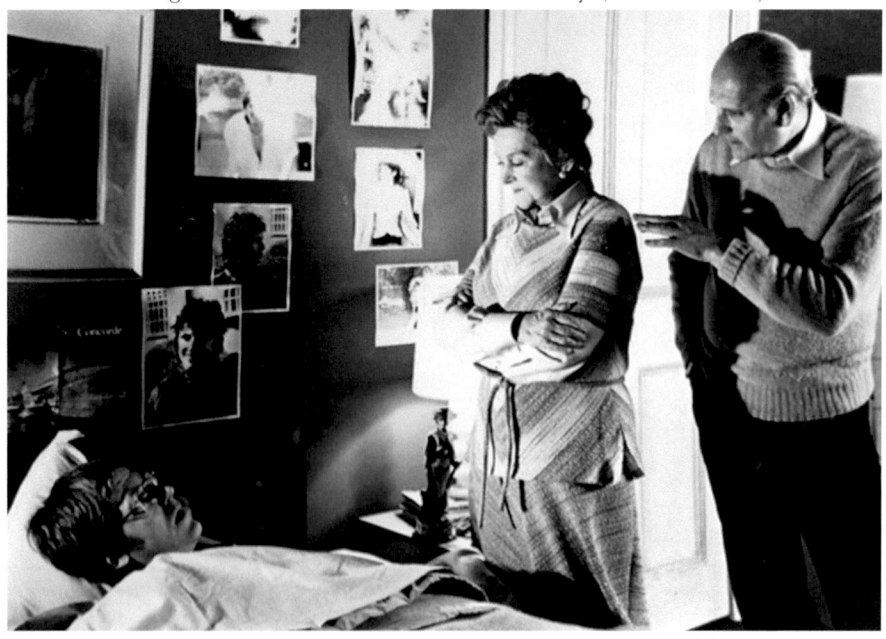

A highlight of *Carry On Emmannuelle* was working with the wonderful Beryl Reid. Here we are rehearsing a scene with director Gerry Thomas. *(Author's Collection)*

CHAPTER 9
The Swinging Sixties

Did you know, dear reader, that I was once in a pop group? Along with my friends Stewart Guidotti, John Sago, Jimmy Luck and Paul Linton, who performed under the name Leslie Tausig. Stewart was our singer, I played the piano and flute, Jimmy was our drummer and Paul and John were on guitars. We met and rehearsed in the Corona Theatre, thanks to Rona Knight who liked to encourage her ex-students. We agreed on the name 'Method' for the group, as some of us were pretend actors. A good name at the time, which I think is what got us going really.

Paul was an enthusiastic 'go-ahead' kind of guy and far too quickly he got us a gig to play at a wedding, after we had been together for about a month. It was a disaster. We only had a couple of numbers of our own, after which we had to busk a few others. Of course after about twenty minutes, we had no choice but to start our rather limited repertoire all over again. This encouraged wedding guests to start asking us for requests, which of course we didn't know how to play! We could only have performed for about half an hour, at which point we were swiftly given our cards!

Paul then got us an interview with the record producer Bunny Lewis, who at that time was one of the big music managers in London. The five of us went to his office in

Denmark Street and played him the four songs we had written and he said he'd like to record them! As I was the only one of us who had a very basic grasp of how to read music, I tried my best to put down all the dots for the man who was going to arrange the music. But needless to say it wasn't good enough, so we put down a little tape recording of ourselves playing these numbers. Bunny then told us that we would have an orchestra backing us, as he didn't want our limited musicianship to bugger it up! When we got to the studio to record our vocals, I couldn't believe who were playing for us... The guitarists were Jimmy Page and Jimmy Sullivan, with Kenny Clare on drums, Peter Snell on the harp, plus saxes, a bass and piano player. I was astounded by this amazing arrangement, and what a sound these professionals produced for us five incompetents. Something else I couldn't believe was the contract that Bunny Lewis offered us, where we would share 2.5% of profits between us, while he would net the other 97.5% Absolutely true! Needless to say we turned it down.

Later on in 1965, Bunny said that a new up-and-coming singer called David Essex wanted to record a version of our song 'Baby I Don't Mind', which I think was our worst. It went out as the B-side on his second ever single, 'Can't Nobody Love You'. This was a flop and failed to chart, though one reviewer commented that the B-side was better. We didn't receive a penny in royalties. Method soon disappeared into the ether and I was never destined to become a sex symbol.

It was thanks to my Auntie Joyce that I got to show my first interest in music. At their house in Chiswick, Joyce and Reg had a small grand piano upstairs in their living room. Every time we visited, I used to love going upstairs and tinkling about on this wonderful instrument. Joyce then paid for me to have a

THE SWINGING SIXTIES

year of piano lessons, for which I am eternally grateful. Once a week at Joyce's house, a teacher would come over, whose name I sadly now can't remember, but she was very patient with me. I had no excuses either, because by then we had an upright piano at home. Perhaps because I didn't practice enough, Joyce stopped paying for the lessons, though by now I was going to Corona, so I already had plenty on my plate to enjoy. Though as soon as I had lost my piano teacher, I started playing more and more on our old upright at home. I found I had a good ear and could pick out a tune with my limited technique. It was my Mum who introduced me to jazz; she enjoyed Fats Waller and the Ink Spots, while my personal favourite at the time was Cab Calloway. I would listen intently and try to copy their tunes on my piano, spending hours trying to find the chords to fit the songs. I found 12-bar blues fun and easy to play, albeit badly!

Another big musical influence came via Tony Ford, a former Corona student who was now working there as a drama teacher in between his acting work. Tony would often help us learn pieces from various plays for our end of term exams at LAMDA. Tony was also of a jazz persuasion and he played the bass. He knew that I had tried to play the piano, so he invited me to his house where he and his wife, also an ex Corona pupil, had a piano. He tried to teach me new chords and how they gave a much different effect on how a tune would sound. I remember Richard O'Sullivan came along once or twice and we loved jamming at Tony's house. They were great times.

In 1956, I discovered Shelly Manne and his Men, a West Coast quintet. They had a hit with the theme tune for the TV series *Peter Gunn*, which I think was the first LP I ever bought. This led me to many more musicians I really enjoyed, and it wasn't long before Richard O'Sullivan and I discovered

Miles Davis and we played the *Kind of Blue* album until it wore out and I had to buy another! For me, this is still the best album ever. I started to hang out with Richard a lot, spending many days having jam sessions at his house, where he had a piano, drums and a Hammond organ. Mrs O was wonderful, bringing us food and drink while we made what must have been a dreadful noise! Richard then bought a vibraphone and a marimba, so we could jam together. They were great days. Two other friends from Corona, Alan Coleshill and Roy Hines (older brother of Frazer) joined us. Roy was a good drummer and Alan bought a bass, despite never having played one before, and he desperately tried to conquer the thing. The four of us started to go to jazz clubs such as Ronnie Scott's, somehow getting in despite being underage.

We very rarely played for others, but once we were asked to perform at one of Rona Knight's events at the Chiswick Town Hall, with Valerie Buckley singing 'I'll Remember April', a jazz classic. I don't think it was the audience's scene, but I think we got away with it. Many years later in December 1974, we all reunited to perform this song as a surprise for Richard during the recording of his *This Is Your Life*. At the time I was back working at Stratford E15 on another Ken Hills production, *Is Your Doctor Really Necessary*. I pleaded with Ken to let me do Richard's *This Is Your Life*, to which he agreed as it was to be recorded early afternoon at Euston Studios and I would be away by 4pm, leaving plenty of time to get back to Stratford for the 7.30pm performance.

I had to be at Euston by 10am to rehearse the show and also record the music, as we had to mime on the night. We had our first rehearsal with host Eamonn Andrews, who would introduce us to a stand-in for Richard, who was not yet at the studio and at this time still not aware of his surprise. We were behind a curtain and the music of 'I'll Remember April' started playing as Eamonn read from his script, hidden of course in the famous big red book, announcing, "Here are your friends from Corona; Valerie Walsh, Roy Hines, Alan Coleshill and Larry Dawn!" DAWN?? Eamonn would then ask Richard if he wanted to play with us, followed by an ad lib on the night, then the three of us would go to our seats. Simple. After the rehearsal, I went to the stage manager to explain that my name is Larry DANN not Dawn. He looked at the script and said, "That's what the script says, I will tell Eamonn". About an hour later we had another rehearsal of the same set up and once again Eamonn announced me as Larry Dawn... I flagged this with the stage manager again, though he said he knew what had happened and told me not to worry.

Now this is where things started to get tricky. Richard arrived at about 3pm and was put in a room well away from all the guests who were to appear. We were literally locked away in another room so we couldn't accidentally bump into him and spoil the surprise. But we were then advised that the final guest, Trevor Howard, was not here yet, meaning we could not start the recording. It wasn't for another three hours that we got the news that Mr Howard had now arrived, but he was drunk and they were plying him with plenty of coffee to get him ready. I was now in panic mode and I asked to see the director of the programme to explain that I had to leave very soon, as I did not have an understudy back at Stratford. I was told that a taxi was waiting for me and that as soon as I'd finished my bit, rather than go to my seat, I was to walk straight out through the audience and into my taxi. The recording finally started at 6.30pm and we were called to the studio. We were called on about 15 minutes into the show and big surprise, Eamonn Andrews once again introduced me as "Larry Dawn", though this time the real Richard was there and kindly corrected him "DANN!" We finished and I rushed through the audience to the front of the studio and there was my taxi waiting for me.

What a driver this man was. It was now about 7pm and he had 30 minutes to get me to the theatre. No mobile phones in those days, so I couldn't even let them know that I was on my way. I swear we went through so many red lights and it was 7.30pm when we got to the Stratford roundabout. In his haste, he drove straight into the back of another vehicle, and there was an almighty crash. "Run!" he said, and I sprinted the last hundred yards or so to go on foot, leaving him to exchange details with the driver of the other vehicle, who thankfully wasn't hurt. I got to the theatre and there was Ken Hill, standing on the pavement in my costume with script in hand, desperately hoping I would turn up. Ken was prepared to go on for me, but as the curtain had already gone up, I literally walked on stage to give my first line, still dressed in my posh *This Is Your Life* gear as I'd not had time to change. As you can imagine, Ken was understandably not happy with me, but we got away with it. After the performance, once my adrenaline had come back down to earth, I thought about that taxi driver and what an amazing thing he had done for me! I hope he didn't get any fines for going through all those red lights or overtaking when he shouldn't have, and what about the damage to his taxi and the car he crashed into? Thank you Sir, the theatre owes you a lot for saving that audience from seeing poor Ken's performance.

The fact that Method hadn't launched my career as a pop star didn't bother me too much, as I can't remember being out of work for too long throughout the 'Swinging Sixties'. On television I appeared in series like *Pardon the Expression* with the brilliant Arthur Lowe, *No Hiding Place* starring Raymond Francis and I had a nice role in *Sherlock Holmes* with Peter Cushing playing the great detective. I also did a lot of touring and in 1968 I was invited back for a revival of *Oh, What a Lovely War* with Brian Murphy directing, assisted by Kevin Palmer. We were to open at the Theatre Royal in Stratford and then go on a tour starting in Oxford.

 A few of the original cast members returned and I was also able to get my then girlfriend Seretta Wilson a part. She had been a student at Corona and I was confident in promoting her to Brian. She didn't let me down. We did very well at E15, getting good reviews as expected, but something wasn't right with the tour that was to follow. We had Oxford and Brighton booked, but then nothing else, so it was decided that we would do a pantomime at a small venue just off the Euston Road called The Place. We had in fact done this same panto when the original *Lovely War* was at Wyndham's, performed as matinees only… Joan really liked to make her actors work!

 In our revival of this panto, Seretta was to play Cinderella and I was to be one of the Ugly Sisters. We were rehearsing the script on our first night in Oxford, where Seretta and I had agreed to share a room in a B&B, booked in the name of Mr & Mrs Dann. But we got off to a very embarrassing start when there was a knock on the door and a woman's voice asked, "Is there a Miss Seretta Wilson in there, because your father is on the phone!" We both went cold. Seretta went downstairs to take the call, came back up a few minutes later and said that her father was coming up to Oxford to collect her and take her straight home to Ealing, meaning she would have to commute to Oxford each day.

I made the decision to see the landlady and apologise for the confusion over the names, a big lie which she fully knew I'd made. She was cross with me, "This type of behaviour is not allowed in my establishment!" It must have been about 11pm, so I paid her for the room and we packed our bags. I said I would leave and go back to Chiswick, as Seretta didn't want a scene when her father arrived. Seretta was 20 at the time and I really couldn't understand her father's rather old-fashioned approach. The following day at work the atmosphere between us wasn't good, we had been seeing each other for a couple of years and I'd had no idea that her father was so protective. That was the end of a very nice relationship.

Since 1967, I had been living in a really good flat share, thanks to my great mate Barry Halliday's then girlfriend Jill Moxey, who had invited me to join her and another Corona student, Al Lampert. The three of us shared for about three years and it worked very well. The flat was 62b Sutton Court Road, with three bedrooms, a bathroom and a kitchen, which had a back door exit down a fire escape to the parking area. The building was on the corner of the intersection leading to the Chiswick flyover, so it was busy and noisy, but the flat was neat, clean and not too expensive.

On one sunny Sunday afternoon, Al and I were sitting in the living room, probably not paying much attention to whatever was on TV. Suddenly we noticed a green budgie was sitting outside on the ledge of the window. We both went up to look, and the budgie didn't fly away. So we decided to open up one of the windows and see what would happen... The windows were metal, single glazed ones that didn't really keep out the noise of the traffic. The budgie was about three feet from the opening we had given him, but he didn't move. We wondered why he was sat there, especially with all that noise going on below. We waited for quite some time, but there was no action. I decided to go to the window and put my hand out. Growing up, we'd had a yellow budgie called Bertie that was loved by all. Hopefully my actions would encourage our new friend to enter the flat...

I put my hand out through the window and, lo and behold, he jumped on and I brought him into the room. Al closed the window and the bird almost immediately spoke to us, "Hello, George Burgess." We were amazed, then the bird repeated his greeting, just in case we hadn't heard it the first time. This was the start of a wonderful relationship with us at the flat. I went and retrieved our now unused birdcage from home, as sadly Bertie had long since passed away. I went to the local pet shop and bought seed and a piece of cuttlefish, which budgies love to sharpen their beaks on.

Well, despite all that trouble and effort, George hardly ever went in the cage, except to eat and drink, choosing to spend most of his time in the living room and having the run of the flat. Of course one of the first things we did was to phone the police to report this lost budgie calling itself George Burgess. They didn't believe the story at first, thinking we were a couple of louts having a laugh. In the end they told us to get in touch with the budgie society and they gave us a telephone number to call. We duly did, and they took our details and said they would contact us if anyone came forward.

A few weeks passed and we knew that George was to be the fourth member of 62b! George loved it and he was amazingly clean and incredibly easy to keep. Twice he escaped from the fire exit and sat in a large tree that dominated the area. After causing Al, Jill and I some mild panic, he decided he would come back to the warmth of home. George enjoyed watching TV by sitting on the frame of my glasses and we particularly enjoyed a very popular American comedy show called *Rowan & Martin's Laugh-In*. One of the catchphrases of this programme was "Sock it to me, baby", which I taught George to say very quickly, along with many other silly things. He was a great learner and a brilliant bird, what a huge joy to live with him.

We rarely had parties at the flat, as it was sort of in the contract not to make any nuisance. But we did once throw a little soirée for our friend Huw Halliday (no relation to Barry) who was getting married. We gave him a stag night to remember, with plenty of beer and three naughty films. I had a projector with sound, as I had in the past tried to make short films on 8mm, though I was very unsuccessful as it was so hard to edit them. Also joining the stag party were Al, Barry and Stewart Guidotti. Poor Jill was banished, though she perfectly understood. Plenty of beer was consumed before the showing and we were ready for a little titillation… but the first film was so disgusting that Huw threw up all over the carpet, having never made the loo! We didn't bother with the other two. Not the greatest stag do, but Huw got to his wedding and now lives in Australia.

Not that it had anything to do with this stag effort, but Al decided to move out, as he was going to live with his lovely girlfriend Kathy. To keep the Corona incest going, we invited another former student to take over Al's room. Enter Anne Kettle, who naturally we nicknamed 'Teapot'. At the time, Anne was going out with Thane Bettany, who had taught me drama at Corona. We had worked together on what I thought was a good production of *The Long and the Short and the Tall* and so I was delighted when Thane asked me to go to Sweden for a production of *The Taming of the Shrew* he was directing. We were to open the play at the National Theatre of Sweden and then tour the country, playing mostly one day at a time in schools and other theatres around the south of Sweden for three months. I was given a nice house to stay in on the outskirts of Stockholm, which I shared with three others from the cast; Michael Des Barres, who later became an actor and rock star in the USA; Stewart Bevan, who had also been at Corona and enjoyed a long career on stage and screen; and June Brown who of course would become best known for playing Dot Cotton in *EastEnders*. June was to play Katherine, while I was playing her father, which I hope worked despite me being thirteen years younger than her. June was excellent and was also a wonderful matriarch to us all.

I was dubious of going away for so long and basically playing schools, sometimes on early mornings, but I really enjoyed it. Many a time you could see students following the script, checking that we had got all of Shakespeare's lines right! We had a Luton lorry and a minibus to travel in. The scenery was made up of three easy to set up three-sided screens, which swivelled on casters for scene changes. As the cast, we were responsible for the setting up and dismantling, which was basically down to me, Stewart and Michael (known to us as Mickey). The three of us would usually travel together in the Luton and quite often we would have a gig miles from Stockholm, so the company would arrange digs for us. I stayed in some lovely homes, usually owned by people who were connected with the venue we were playing.

OH, WHAT A LOVELY MEMOIR

Despite my initial reservations, *The Taming of the Shrew* was a very enjoyable job. On one occasion we were stationed in Malmo, just across the water from Copenhagen. We were there for the weekend and having the Sunday off, we decided to take the ferry across to have a look at the city. We noticed a poster saying that Jimi Hendrix was playing in the theatre at the Tivoli Gardens. I knew the drummer from 'the Experience', Mitch Mitchell, who was also with us at Corona. As it was now latish afternoon, I suggested we went and found the Tivoli Gardens and I would try and see if Mitch was able to say hello. I found the stage door and asked for Mitch, who lo and behold eventually came to the door and invited us in. Amazing. The three of us followed him to their dressing room and there were Jimi Hendrix and Noel Redding! Unbelievable. Mitch introduced me and I then brought in Mickey and Stewart and we stayed for a while and chatted. Jimi was charming, no front to him, they talked about where they were going next and we explained our tour, though it was not quite as exotic. Noel Redding hardly said a word, instead he sat in a corner strumming a guitar. I suppose for a bass player that might make a relaxing change? Mitch kindly asked if we wanted to stay for the concert, but we really couldn't, as we sadly had to get the ferry back. What a disappointment. Still my kudos went sky high, not only with Mickey and Stewart, but with the rest of the company when we went back and told them. Hendrix tragically died only a year later in Kensington, aged 27.

On one occasion I was driving the Luton on another long trip, with Thane Bettany sat next to me. We were chatting about the past and our Corona days when he suddenly said that he was in love. Oh dear, I hoped he meant Anne? He then said I would meet them when we got to the theatre... A difficult situation, but I didn't say anything. We arrived and I was introduced to this young man. I honestly had no idea of Thane's sexuality. Now I was in a dilemma, what would I say to Anne when I returned to London? We finished the contract in the September and travelled back, this time by boat rather than plane as I think they ran out of money. Back at the flat, I decided to do what I thought was the right thing and tell Anne, who was absolutely furious with me. They later married and had a son called Paul, now a highly successful actor himself.

As well as there now being quite an atmosphere between Anne and myself at the flat, there was also a noticeable absence. During my twenty-week tour of Sweden, George had escaped once again, only this time he had never returned. I admit that when I found there were a lot of tears, he was my best friend at the time and gave me so many fun memories. Our hope was that having got to his favourite tree, a larger bird hadn't got him and that instead he had flown to another address and said, "Hello, George Burgess" to a new family.

I didn't have much time to grieve, as I was soon asked to go up to Lancaster and join a company that was touring the North with two plays, *The Venetian Twins* by Goldoni and Shakespeare's *Pericles*. A number of us in this cast liked to play the card game bridge, and we did spend an awful lot of our time when we weren't on stage, playing cards backstage. Once when we were performing at the Cambridge Arts Theatre, I got up to go back on and one of the backstage boys said, "I'll sit in for you, if you like?" That was how I met my future *The Bill* co-star Tony Scannell. I suggested he join us for the rest of the tour, as our ASM was moving on after Cambridge and we didn't have a replacement. Tony readily agreed and was a bloody good ASM and an even better bridge player!

OH, WHAT A LOVELY MEMOIR

I will always remember when we did a one-night performance in Wigan. We arrived at the theatre, which had seen better days, and we wondered when it had last seen an audience. We were told that bookings were not good. Never mind, we got the scenery for *Pericles* set up and went to get a snack somewhere local. We came back and got our makeup and costumes ready, only to be told that there were only seven people waiting to watch. The rule in theatre is that you don't have to perform if there are fewer in the audience than actors on stage. There were nine of us, but having travelled from Lancaster to Wigan, it seemed ridiculous not to go ahead, so we did. After two and a half hours of Shakespeare, we came to take our bows and got a standing ovation for at least a minute from those seven people in the audience. Wonderful, I had tears in my eyes. I am very proud of the work that company did.

As this famous decade drew to a close, it did so in such spectacular fashion. Ask anyone of my vintage where they were when man landed on the Moon and I'm sure they will be able to tell you in vivid detail! I'll never forget staying up all night in the flat to watch the live broadcast on 20 July 1969. It must have been about 3.30am our time when the event happened. Mum had come over to watch with me and at the exact moment when, in a fuzzy black and white picture, Neil Armstrong took that last step from the ladder and landed on the surface of the Moon and said, "That's one small step for man, one giant leap for mankind", my mother let out an enormous snore, having fallen asleep. That moment of history is now emblazoned on my mind and every time I hear that phrase, I laugh. I thank Mum for this memory.

CHAPTER 10

Hitting The Big Time

The Sixties were an amazing time for me, with lots of parties and plenty of work in the theatre. Towards the end of the decade, after a few years' absence from the big screen, I started landing the occasional film role. I got a surprise one day in 1969 when Hazel actually phoned me for a change. Usually it was the other way round, with me calling to ask if there was anything going? She told me I had been cast in a new film for a Spanish director called José Ramón Larraz, and that I had been offered "a very nice part". Like a fool, I believed her...

I had still not been sent a script when Hazel phoned to say I needed to be on location at pub in the middle of nowhere, somewhere in Wiltshire, the following morning by 7.30am. I of course got there on time and introduced myself to José, who replied in broken English. I discovered very soon that he had a fairly light grasp of our language. I hung around in this pub for an age until eventually a crew arrived and set up. I was told by the assistant director that I was to play a barman, and that two actors playing a young couple would come to the bar and ask me for coffee. I explained that pubs did not sell coffee, which at the time was a fact. He replied, "It doesn't matter, that's what the director wants." I took my place behind the bar and looked for any coffee making implements, but there were none, only two cups and saucers that had been placed with nothing in them down by the pumps. The two young actors then arrived, the man in high fashion and the girl with barely anything on. I then realised what kind of film this was! A rehearsal was called and on "Action!" the man came and said "two coffees" and walked away. I replied by saying absolutely nothing, as I could hardly yell, "pubs don't do coffee, piss off!" They shot the scene immediately and after only one take, "Cut!" was called and that was it, I could go home! I asked what was this film was called and was told it was *She Died With Her Boots On... and Not Much Else*. I think I got £50 for my "very nice part"... Thanks Hazel! Months later I was in Piccadilly Circus and saw a large poster for the film. I couldn't believe it and so I bought a ticket and must have been the only punter not wearing a dirty mackintosh. When the titles for this dreadful film came up, I had third billing, my best ever on the big screen!

    Another exciting film role came in 1969 when I was cast in *The Body Stealers* starring Patrick Allen and George Sanders. The film was about RAF pilots mysteriously disappearing and Patrick Allen's character had to find out why. I played his sergeant, driving him around in a Land Rover. I had a few weeks playing this "Yes Sir, No Sir" part, with plenty of time off. I arrived on my first day at Beaconsfield Studios for costume and makeup, before a car would take me to location at Northolt Airport. An assistant came to me and asked if I would mind if Mr Sanders shared my car? Wow I thought, *he's* sharing *my* car? I of course said that I would be delighted. I got to the driveway and couldn't believe that it was a Rolls-Royce! I realised fairly quickly that it was really *me* sharing *his* car.

I jumped in the front with the driver and eventually Mr Sanders arrived and sat in the back. I very politely said hello, but got no reply and the journey to the airport was not a time for conversation. Later on in the shoot I was parked in my Land Rover, probably 50 yards away from the rest of the unit, on the grass where I went when I wasn't needed. I was reading the paper when I looked across and saw George Sanders walking towards me very slowly. I wondered where he could be going? He got closer and closer and I got more and more confused. He opened the passenger door, got in and sat beside me, without saying a word. At this point I have been on the film for several weeks and he has completely ignored me. "Nice day?" I said, but as usual there was no reply. I tried something else like "Aren't we lucky with the weather?" Still nothing. I got back to my reading, as I could think of nothing else to say to this man, who had been a big star in his day. Many minutes of silence passed until he got out of the vehicle and slowly walked back to where he'd come from. I can find no explanation for this event!

Later on at Beaconsfield Studios, I was parked up in the driveway at the front entrance, awaiting a cue on my radio for 'Action'. I then had to drive at speed around the corner of said building to pick up Patrick Allen. Whilst waiting, I noticed another Rolls-Royce parked behind me. I thought nothing of this, until the driver got out and told me in no uncertain terms that I must get out of his way. I explained that I was waiting for an 'Action' to drive off, and I knew that the second I got out of his way that 'Action' would be called and I would mess up the take. The driver insisted, saying, "Mr Brynner has to leave!" I turned to look at the Roller and lo and behold there was Yul Brynner. But I felt my need was greater than that of the Oscar-winning actor and I repeated my first reply to the now panicking Roller driver. Fortunately 'Action' was called and I drove off into the shot, leaving the angry King of Siam behind. When I saw *The Body Stealers*, I wasn't given a character name and was credited as Larry Dan! It's strange how often producers don't seem to realise that when you misspell an actor's name, it offends.

My greatest film experience of the decade came earlier in 1968, when Hazel told me I had an audition with Maude Spector, probably the queen of casting agents, for a film to be shot in Austria - a big deal. I was given all the details for my audition, which was to take place at one of those posh offices in Golden Square. Come the day and there were a few other guys of my age there, some of whom I knew, all sitting as if waiting for a doctor's appointment. I got my call to go through to the casting room and there was Maude, whom I had never met before, who introduced me to J. Lee Thompson, the Oscar-nominated director of *The Guns of Navarone*. Maude told him how good I was and praised me to the heavens, which had never happened to me before at a casting, nor since come to that! Mr Thompson revealed very little and I left the room not knowing anything about the film or what part he wanted to see me for. I left in a bit of a haze, got the tube back to Chiswick and phoned Hazel to see if there was any news. "Not yet dear", which was her usual reply. I was never convinced that she ever actually followed up on any of her clients' auditions.

But miracles do happen and it was probably the following day when she phoned again to tell me I had got the film. It was called *Before Winter Comes*, they were sending me a script and I would be engaged for eight weeks, filming in Austria for the entire shoot. Wow! The money was more per week than I had ever earned before and on top of this, I would also get £10 a day expenses. That doesn't sound like much now, but when you consider my recent experience in New York where I'd had to pay for my own lodgings out of my fee, having an extra £70 a week to play with was enormous for a young actor in 1968.

I was to play a squaddie in the British Army called Al, stationed in Austria after the Second World War. My character was there to help with the repatriation of prisoners back to their countries. The film was to star David Niven, Topol, Anna Karina and a young John Hurt in his first leading film role. More details came through which revealed we were to be flown to Munich, where we would be collected by chauffeur and driven to the five-star Hotel Bristol in Salzburg. Fantastic! The script arrived, which I read and discovered that I had very little to do, just the occasional line to say, so not much to study. I was used to playing small parts in most of the films I had already been in, so that was no change. But this was the first time I was to travel abroad with a large film unit, and going First Class would be a real bonus.

It was early April 1968 when I packed my bags and was collected by a chauffeur driving a very smart car. Arriving at Heathrow, I found the British Airways desk, where there was an assistant to meet me. After all the formalities of passport and customs checks, I was taken to the First Class lounge. In there waiting were the other five young actors who had been cast to play the rest of the squaddies; George Innes, Tony Selby, Hugh Futcher, Colin Spaull and Christopher Sandford, who was the only one I vaguely knew as we had both been at Corona Academy together. Also there was John Collin, who was to play our sergeant in the film.

What followed in my First Class lounge debut was a lot of alcohol abuse, which helped to break the ice for all us squaddies getting to know each other. Then onto the plane we marched, where we abused our livers further. I don't remember much of that flight. We arrived in Munich to be met by two chauffeurs, driving plush Mercedes. It was a long journey to Salzburg and I remember us all needing to stop for a break. Of course, we had stopped at a place where we could have another drink. I was not a big drinker and was soon very much the worse for wear. Drink makes you say the most stupid things and I remember telling John Collin, a stocky man, how I was very good at Aikido, a Japanese martial art that I had been studying for over a year at the BBC club. I explained how it worked and what I could do. Eventually we arrived at the Hotel Bristol, and I recall signing in and immediately going to my room, where I collapsed into a long, deep sleep.

The next thing I remember was waking up the following morning, thankfully without any hangover. The film company had an office in the hotel where I had to go and collect my expenses, already exchanged into Austrian schillings. The exchange rate at this time was very much in our favour, meaning our expenses would go even further. I was also given a schedule, where I found that I wouldn't be needed for a few days and so my time was my own. In fact, it looked like I only had eight days' work across the whole eight weeks! I already knew from the script that I had very few lines; George and Tony seemed to have most of them, so I embraced the situation. I had lots of cash and loads of free time to spend it in. I'd already had my costume fitted in London, so now had absolutely nothing to do but enjoy Salzburg for a few days. This gig was going to be a doddle!

HITTING THE BIG TIME

I met up with some of the guys for a late breakfast, where they explained that Hugh Futcher had been attacked in the night by John Collin, who had mistaken him for me and challenged him to defend himself using his Aikido skills! Poor Hugh, who was eight stone soaking wet, had been jumped on by all fourteen stone of John Collin whilst he was looking for the loo in the hotel corridor! We were all very pissed.

A few of us felt that staying in the Hotel Bristol for the entirety of the shoot was not really for us. We learned that the filming location was about 45km away in a village called Abtenau, so we decided to find somewhere a little quieter to stay on the way there. We ended up in a village about 9km from Salzburg called Anif, staying in the Hotel Friesacher. This excellent hotel also came with the Friesacher Stadl, a nightclub disco with a bar. Perfect! It was owned by the Friesacher family and the main man, Mr Friesacher, couldn't have been more helpful, no doubt as we were spending a lot of cash there! One day he told me that if I saw his elderly father to please not think anything bad of him... I had no idea what he meant, as up to then I hadn't even known about his father, let alone seen him.

A few days later I was arriving back at the hotel and coming down the stairs came the spitting image of Adolf Hitler! I immediately understood what Mr Friesacher had meant, his father was a very elderly man who was very clearly a Nazi sympathiser; he had the same moustache and hair cut as Hitler, and was even wearing a soldier's uniform, possibly his original one. Mr Friesacher suddenly appeared and rapidly took him away out of sight, back to whichever part of the hotel he had escaped from. I only saw him this once and none of the other actors ever saw him. Extraordinary.

OH, WHAT A LOVELY MEMOIR

At first, the six of us squaddies did things together. I remember us taking a cable car to the top of the mountain just a little walk from the hotel. It might have been April, but it was warm enough for us to take our shirts off and sunbathe. After a few days of this paid holiday, we all started to form our own little groups and split up for our own adventures, as you do. I became good mates with Colin and Hugh, while George and Tony did their own thing. I have no idea what Christopher did, as he didn't seem to hang out with any of us.

Eventually, the time came where I would actually have to go to work. An early call was followed by a quick breakfast and a Merc waiting for me outside the hotel. I seemed to be the only one. After about a half-hour drive, I arrived in Abtenau, stopping at a hotel that was being used as our makeup and costume base. I was met by an assistant and asked to get my costume on and then go to makeup. I duly did this and when I entered the makeup room, there already seated in the chair was David Niven! Just me and one of the biggest film stars in the world, waiting for our makeup. I bumbled something like, "Oh, hello Mr Niven". He replied warmly, "David. What's your name?" I told him and he smiled, "OK, Larry Boy", and that became my nickname for the entire shoot, 'Larry Boy'. What a lesson in how to greet and relax a fellow artist in one brilliant swoop. I have never forgotten that and from that day forward I have tried to do the same for any actor who has arrived with nerves on their first day. Thank you David, I hope I followed your example well.

We chatted for a while before David was called to the set. I followed soon afterwards, as my makeup consisted of a bit of powder and an occasional continuity hair cut. The location was a little car ride away, to an area that had been made into a prisoner of war army base, with many wooden buildings created to hold prisoners and barracks for us soldiers. I didn't know a soul on the set, but I was given a lot of respect, possibly because I was what is known as a 'featured artiste'. This particular featured artiste spent most of his time in the background pretending to know what he was doing. Mr J. Lee Thompson announced via his first assistant director, Jake Wright, that he wanted his artiste, which on this occasion was me. I don't think I ever had a conversation directly with Mr Thompson, though I certainly watched him work. He had a habit of being given sheets of paper by his PA and then tearing them into little strips. By the end of a scene, there would be a large amount of A4 paper in shreds surrounding his feet!

I can't remember what I did on that first day, not very much I suspect. I think the others had arrived and we were placed somewhere in the background, pretending to organise the extras who were playing prisoners and pushing them around. It was a big film with hundreds of extras. Of course, we didn't speak German and only a few of them spoke a little English. None of us really knew what was happening, but no one seemed to mind. After I was released on my first day, I got the car back to the Friesacher and I now had many days off, with plenty of time to spend our wonga in the Stadl. Hugh and I liked to play cards and we tried to get a card school going as we both liked a little gamble. Sadly this never happened in Austria, but when we got back to Blighty, Hugh arranged card schools in Wandsworth, which became quite lucrative for me for a while.

Colin Spaull and I spent a lot of time together, particularly in the disco next door. When we had a long weekend off during the shoot because of a national holiday, we decided to drive to Vienna for the weekend, a long way from Anif, but worth it! I hired a car from one of the drivers, who said I was insured. I didn't question him and luckily nothing arose from it. We booked a hotel for one night and hit the town, visiting places like the big Ferris wheel that had famously featured in the Orson Welles movie *The Third Man*, and the Schönbrunn Palace, where we bumped into Jake Wright, our first assistant director. He was with a woman we were told not to mention, so I won't... what happens in Vienna, stays in Vienna. Colin and I also ended up in some dodgy bar where we were accosted by girls. No way would our expenses have covered that!

Back in Anif, one night after drinking too many cocktails in the Stadl, Colin and I decided to go to the zoo, which was only a few hundred yards up the road. We had visited it before during the day, but when we got there this time it was well after midnight and unsurprisingly we found it closed! Not to be put off, these two totally pissed actors decided to climb over the wrought iron gates and wander around our own personal zoo until the early hours. When I think of this now, I shudder to think what would have happened had we been caught. We would certainly have lost our parts in the film and possibly faced a huge fine that no expenses would have covered.

Right down one end of the zoo was an area for all the big cats; tigers, lions and other very dangerous animals. Well, being an idiot, I decided to climb over the security rails to get right up close to the bars of the male lion's enclosure. I could feel his breath on me, why he didn't give me a smack in the chops with his giant paw I will never know. Anyway, I got away with it and we went back to the gates and climbed back out. It was probably about 3am. The following morning, or possibly afternoon by the time we got up, Colin and I made a vow not to mention this to anyone, as we realised the penalty if it was discovered. Thankfully we have kept this secret until now! The most stupid thing I have ever done. I seem to recall that I never drank that much again on the rest of the shoot.

A follow up to this story is that as I was feeling flash with too much cash in my pocket, I invited my mother and my flatmate Jill Moxey to come over and visit for a week. I paid for their tickets and booked them a room at the hotel. Over they came and I took them onto the set, where I introduced them to David Niven, who as you can imagine was charm itself. My Mum was in heaven. I then took them sightseeing in the car, first a trip to Berchtesgaden, Hitler's retreat, followed by a drive to Austria's highest peak at the Grossglockner. On the long drive back down, my brakes heated up to the point where they failed and wouldn't work. I had to rely on the hand brake for the rest of the way and we eventually got back having descended at a ridiculously slow pace.

I then took them to the zoo in Anif, during opening hours this time! We wandered around and eventually got to the lion's cage. I hadn't mentioned anything to Mum about my ridiculous adventure with Colin. There were many of us looking at the male lion, the very one that I'd had a drunken conversation with. He walked up to the bars, turned his back on us and with amazing accuracy urinated all over me. No one else was hit, just me! He had remembered. I got the biggest laugh ever and stank like hell. Thankfully the hotel was close at hand.

When writing this, I still can't believe I did all this without spending a penny over my expenses. In fact, Colin and I went into Salzburg and both of us bought an Omega Seamaster watch and had two jackets made, one in suede and one in leather. We even had parties at the Lee Electric boys' place over there. On one occasion I was driven to one of their parties by a German member of the crew, whose name now escapes me. He had a very fast sports car and insisted that he drive me back to the Friesacher. But by now he was totally pissed and I should have known better. I have never been so frightened in my life as we raced along a twenty-mile stretch of mountain passes. Yet another ridiculous adventure I got away with.

One of the joys of being on set was the lunches, as we had fantastic caterers on location. The production had erected a giant tent lined with rows of tables. The first line was for the stars; David Niven, Topol, Anna Karina and John Hurt, as well J. Lee Thompson, Gilbert Taylor the DOP and a few others. On the second table were us, the 'Artistes'. This posh seating arrangement meant that I didn't know who was on the third table, let alone the tenth. It was really pretentious. Joining Topol on the top table were a couple of his friends who had parts in the film. Sadly, he never wanted to enjoy our company, as I understand he was very wary of being in Austria, especially doing a film about the Nazis. In fact when he arrived for the production, he refused to fly into Munich and had to be flown into a small airport near the location.

I thought Topol was a fine actor who had a magnetic presence on stage. I saw his *Fiddler on the Roof* many times as my great friend Maurice Lane was in it. Sadly, David Niven did not get on with Topol. In fact, he wouldn't or couldn't sit at the table with him, choosing instead to sit with us. One day, David explained that it was because of Topol's eating habits.

"Look at him," he said, "eating with his hands". We looked and sure enough that was how he was eating his meal. He also told us that Topol had said to him, "I have learned the technique of looking into the camera lens after each line, just like you do..." David was not happy with this insult. "I've never done that", he said. It was great having David on our table, listening to his stories in the way only he could tell them.

One day he said to me "What are you doing tonight, Larry Boy?" "Nothing, David", I said. "Would you like to come and have dinner with Hjördis and me?" I think you can guess my answer, dear reader. What a wonderful night I had with David and his wife in a fantastic restaurant in Salzburg, listening to this legend tell so many stories. There was me, an overpaid background artiste having the time of my life, wanting to tell him that as a boy, I had been an extra on a film called *Happy Ever After* he had made at Elstree with Yvonne De Carlo in 1954. I didn't, but I now wish I had because he would have told me even more stories. He was a wonderful man and I feel hugely privileged to have worked with him.

There is a tradition that at the end of filming, when the movie is 'in the can' as they say, the star of the film will give a little party for 'important' guests. Well, when we had finished, David organised a trip to the lakes for literally everyone who had worked on the film. He had personally arranged the many coaches that were needed, the hotel where we had drinks and a meal, as well as trips on the river. I seem to remember Tony Selby getting very drunk and diving off the boat for a swim. It was very cold in that water, even though we were now in June. Tony sobered up very quickly! David spent the whole time making sure everyone had what they wanted. It was a day to remember for so many of us, I believe there might have been nearly a hundred people there. Despite being invited, Topol did not join us and I'm sorry to say chose to throw his own party instead, but only for his friends. That sums him up for me.

I have never been cast in a film like *Before Winter Comes* again, but I enjoyed every second of being on big wages, with plenty of time off and far too much alcohol. Wonderful. When I got home, I had my wages to spend, which I should have put down as a deposit on a house, but instead I spent a large amount on a car that I'd always wanted, a Gilbern. What, you may ask? The Gilbern was the only car made in Wales, built out of fibreglass with an MGB engine. These were two hundredweight lighter than the average car and they went like a rocket. I loved driving this marvellous car and going on tour with it was a pleasure. I can now admit that after one Saturday night performance at the Leeds Playhouse, I drove back to Chiswick in one hour forty-five minutes. The M1 was fairly new then, but I'll leave you to work out how fast I was going!

After *Before Winter Comes* hit UK cinemas in January 1969, it seemed to unlock a steady stream of squaddie roles for me. Later that year, I was cast by John Glenister for an episode of the BBC's prestigious *Thirty-Minute Theatre* series, called *The Victims: Frontier*. I had worked for John a few times before and for once I had the joy of not having to go to a casting audition! The play was written by Don Shaw, and alongside me the cast included David Barry, who went on to play Frankie Abbott in *Please Sir!* and the follow up series *The Fenn Street Gang*; and another up-and-coming actor called Tom Baker, who of course went onto enjoy huge success when he became the fourth *Doctor Who*. Even before he played the famous Time Lord, Tom was a wonderfully eccentric and larger-than-life character actor.

The Victims: Frontier was a drama about a young East German man trying to escape to the West, trapped in No Man's Land having hurt himself by jumping over the wall. David played the trapped man, while Tom was a corporal to my lieutenant as we tried to negotiate to go and get him. It was filmed over a week at the Army training area in Aldershot, all night shooting. It was very cold, especially for David as he had to spend a lot of the time lying on the ground.

During the filming, Don Shaw visited the set quite often. He told me he was writing a new TV play called *Sovereign's Company* based on his time at Sandhurst, the military academy. The script would tell the story of young men from privileged backgrounds going through tough training to become officers. Don explained that the main character was based on his own experience, as a cadet who found himself unsuited to Army life. As fascinating as this was, I wondered why he was telling me all this… It turned out that he wanted me to play him, which was the first time anyone had written a role with me in mind. What an honour! *Sovereign's Company* was made as an episode of *The Wednesday Play* for ITV and, true to his word, Don arranged for me to be cast as the character of Hurt.

The play was shot at Sandhurst in March 1970 and was directed by Alan Clarke, a Liverpudlian who would become famous for making violent films like *Scum* and *Made in Britain*. Because he had no say in my casting, and hadn't even met me before we started filming, I got the impression that he wasn't too happy about my casting. Hard as I tried, I just couldn't hit it off with him, in fact I can hardly remember him saying a word to me. I thought I did a reasonable job for him, though needless to say he never used me again. Not easy, but then they can't all be as easy as making *Before Winter Comes*.

Sightseeing with Colin Spaull and Tony Selby. *(Author's Collection)*

CHAPTER 11
The Road to Rutherford

Being at an all-boys school until I was five, I was not comfortable talking to the opposite sex. I can remember my first crush; a girl who lived round the corner in Burnaby Gardens. I never knew her name, as I never dared ask, but I always looked for her when we were playing. It wasn't long before she disappeared from sight, so she must have moved away. Then when I went to Gunnersbury Prep, I still hadn't come across girls to talk to yet. Next door to us at No. 8 was a girl called Marion Moore, who was about the same age as me. Over time we started to get on well, but then the same thing happened and Marion also disappeared from sight. But unlike my first crush, Marion couldn't have moved away, because I still saw Mr and Mrs Moore coming and going from No. 8. I eventually asked Mum where Marion had gone and she explained that the poor girl had got cancer and had passed away. I think this was my first knowledge of someone I knew dying and it took me a long time to get over that. Marion was nice and I really missed her.

It was around this time that my football chum Tony Wotton and I started talking about girls, as we had both felt something strange happening 'down there'… We used to go up to my bedroom and secretly discuss girls and how we didn't have a clue about what to do. I hope Tony later found his life partner, as I did.

When I got to Corona, there were more girls than boys and I found it quite difficult to talk to any of them, especially wearing those tights and a jockstrap in ballet! When I was thirteen, I was told that a girl fancied me who was not frightened of coming forward... I had no idea how to handle this, even though I knew I wanted to. Trudy was her name and she wore strong perfume, which was another first for me, as I'd only known aunts and grannies wearing that. I inadvertently rejected her by not showing any interest. I fancied two girls at Corona, Carol Oliver and Jennifer Beech. Why two at the same time? Must have been my hormones! This was a huge problem; did I ask them both out? Did I hell! I completely lost my bottle and never told them of my desires, which was probably just as well as I'm sure I would have only said something stupid.

It wasn't until I went to my first party, where we sat around drinking lemonade and having the occasional sausage roll, that Carol arrived. It was soon getting dark and couples started getting together on sofas and chairs, for a cuddle and a kiss. I finally plucked up the courage and bravely asked Carol if she would like to sit with me... and she did! Wow, I had Carol sitting on my lap and literally had my first kiss with her, my dream girl. I think she stayed for quite a while, then she went off with someone else... I was getting the idea of what parties and girls were about, as I sat once again like a gooseberry. I went home dreaming about Carol, knowing that I would see her at school the next day and would be able to chat to her. She ignored me, as if nothing had happened. Brutal!

It was about a year later that I got paired with a girl called Janice in ballet. We were doing double work, where the boy helps support the girl and they perform lifts. You obviously start to get close whilst not wearing too many clothes. I asked Janice if she would like to go to the pictures, and she said yes. I picked her up at her house in Acton and met her parents, then we went off to the cinema just around the corner (I can't remember what we saw!) Then I took her home, where we had our first peck on the doorstep. I had my first girlfriend! Janice and I went out for a couple of years, before she eventually got fed up with me and took off with another boy.

Now that I'd had my first relationship, I had a lot more confidence, so much so that once I remember when Dad was at work and Mum was out, I invited two girls, Valerie and Norma, around for a game of strip poker with me, Roy and Alan. I didn't think the girls would come, but they did. So we played and we eventually got to the important part where I only had my underpants to go, Valerie was down to her bra and knickers and Norma, who evidently didn't play much poker, was topless. Suddenly, we heard the front door open and my Mum shouting, "I'm home". You have never seen five young people get dressed so quickly! Mum knew what was happening, but was very diplomatic and said nothing except, "Would you all like a cup of tea?" Bless her heart.

Many dates and parties later, when I was in my late 20s I fell for Maggie Vieler, who had recently become a student at Corona and really wanted to be a dancer. She travelled from Reading every day, about 40 miles on the bus. We started going out together, though this wasn't too easy with her commute. I asked my Mum if Maggie could stay with us during the week and amazingly she said yes, as long as it was all right with her parents. Fortunately her mother had met me and approved. Maggie was to have my room, while I would sleep in the dining room downstairs. Naturally at around 1am, I would creep upstairs, missing that one creaking step that would have given the game away, sneak into my room and we would... well, I'll leave the rest to your imagination!

We got away with this for quite some time, until Maggie's mother told her that she had to go and live with a friend of the family in Surbiton. Well, it was fun while it lasted! We went for a holiday in Mevagissey with Auntie Joyce and Reg, who being very astute kept us apart at night! That was a fine time though as I was now in the West End doing *Oh, What a Lovely War* and as Maggie was no longer at Corona, we could see each other during the day.

When *Lovely War* ended in the West End, just before we were due to go to New York, the show was invited to Paris for the Theatre of Nations, a regular event where France would invite the best theatre from around the world to appear. I took Maggie with me and we had a great week in gay Paris, where I found a little place for us to stay. Maggie's mother was by now OK with us being together, especially as I would soon be going to the USA and would possibly not see her for many months. It was in my mind to propose to Maggie, but being me I chickened out. I thought of the old adage 'absence makes the heart grow fonder' and decided that when I was back from the States, I would definitely pop the question.

Off I went to the USA and started writing letters home at least twice a week. Gradually, the replies became less romantic, until none arrived at all. I didn't know what to do. I still wrote, asking if all was OK, but never got another reply. When I got back seven months later, I eventually managed to get in touch with her via her mother. Maggie was now living at a new address in Earls Court. I went to see her and she confirmed my fears that she was now seeing someone else, a dancer she had been in a show with. Oh my, it hit me hard and my confidence was now at an all-time low.

I eventually dusted myself off and had many little romances that lasted weeks or months. Then after my relationship with Seretta Wilson ended rather embarrassingly, I continued my search for 'the one'. I met a dancer called Peggy, who was a lovely person and we hit it off. But I hadn't known her for long when she got a job in Italy with a touring company that did musicals, meaning she would be away for many months. After a few weeks, I suggested that I go and stay with her in Bologna for a week or two. We arranged this by letter (no mobile phones in 1968!) I booked a flight to Milan, got a train to Bologna and eventually found her at the theatre she was playing. I stayed with her at her hotel for free, which was great as I was struggling a bit with the cost of all the travelling. But they only had a couple of days left at this venue, before the company were heading off to Livorno. I wanted to go with her, but the 200 mile journey would have cost me a fair few pennies and there was no way I'd have been allowed to travel with Peggy on the company coach. So she arranged for me to get a lift with the man who was driving the lorry carrying all the scenery. I was to meet him at the theatre scene dock at midnight.

Amazingly, there was this giant lorry as promised, with the driver ready and waiting to take me to Livorno. The driver knew about as much English as I did Italian, but I sat with him high up in the cabin and we hit the road. I remember driving through Florence at 4am, it looked beautiful, but we didn't stop. In fact, we did the whole journey in one fell swoop, arriving at our destination sometime around 10am, where Peggy was there to meet me. I remember I was very tired, desperate for a pee and very hungry. Fortunately I got to pee, but sleep had to wait, as we went for a nice meal together. I was very happy and had a great time with her as we spent the next few days wandering around the area, seeing the sights whilst getting to know each other. We even went to Pisa and climbed the leaning tower!

My real reason for going to all this effort was to see if Peggy was the girl for me. I'm not sure if I was desperate to propose after what had happened with Maggie, and even though I had known Peggy for about a year, we had only been seeing each other for a couple of months. My wallet of lira was now almost empty and I had to confess that I would have to go back to England. I had already booked a return flight from Milan, but how was I going to get there? Peggy kindly lent me some money for a train fare and off I went to Milan airport. I didn't propose, I really liked Peggy, but it felt too soon.

An extraordinary thing happened when I got to the airport. As I was waiting for my plane, a couple who had just come off a flight came up to me and said, "Are you Larry?" They introduced themselves as Peggy's parents! I had never met them and I don't believe Peggy and I had even talked much about our families and I certainly hadn't been told that they were coming to Italy to see her. Had I been able to afford to stay on for longer, I imagine my first encounter with them would have been quite different if they'd arrived in Livorno to find me staying with their daughter in her hotel room! Considering that Peggy must have told them that I was going to see her there, I wonder why she didn't say anything to me? I had a lovely week or so with her and we exchanged many letters, until eventually I got the 'Dear John' one, explaining that she was going to marry a dancer from the company. Why was I continually finding myself cuckolded by dancers? I still owe Peggy some lira for my train ticket...

Fast forward to August 1971, when I have not long turned 30 and despite doing my fair share of flirting, have still not found 'The One'. I was appearing at the Leeds Playhouse in a production of Shakespeare's *Twelfth Night*. It was here that I first set eyes on Elizabeth Jane Rutherford. Liz was part of the wardrobe department, situated in a very large room on the top floor of the theatre, where a team of five talented ladies were designing and making the costumes for all productions. This was a full-time and full-on job, as the Playhouse had a new production to put on about every four weeks. I must confess that I visited this part of the theatre far more times than necessary for an actor. I also have to say that it was another of the five designers, Katie Pilcher, who I asked out first, but we didn't spend too long together, as I kept noticing Liz... Would I dare ask her out?

Liz shared a house with another girl from wardrobe called Ray, as well as three others from the Playhouse, which is usually how theatre digs work. Then when one person leaves a production, usually an actor, there is always another standing by in the wings ready to take their place. On Friday nights after the performance, Liz and Ray would organise a spaghetti night and invite a few others to come along, all you had to do was bring a bottle or a flagon of beer. They would then watch the late-night film on TV. I was house sharing with Paul Copley and Natasha Pyne who were otherwise engaged, so when I got the invite from Liz and Ray, I went along. When I started going every Friday night, I used the excuse that the TV I had brought up with me from London was rubbish and couldn't get a proper picture. Whilst this was basically true, I had an ulterior motive...

The group also went to discos, which wasn't really my scene as a jazz fan and I prefer to listen than dance. But as Liz was going, I went along and after one particular disco, I asked Liz if she wanted to go to York with me, which was only a short drive from Leeds. We hopped into my Gilbern GT and that night wandered around the streets of York holding hands. This was the start of our long life together.

I spent nine months at the Leeds Playhouse, playing a lot of wonderful parts that I knew I wouldn't be getting in London. But best of all, I had met Liz! Come the end of May 1972, the season was coming to an end and I would be heading back to London. As I wasn't going to be in the last production, which Liz was designing, it meant I would have to leave for home without Liz. So we agreed that when she finished the last production, I would come and get her and we would find a house, flat or room to share.

At the end of June, I went back to Leeds and we filled my Gilbern GT with all of Liz's things. I have no idea how we got everything into such a small car. Our first destination was Suffolk, where my cousins Barbara and Rita were having a double wedding. Liz was to meet the Dann clan for the first time! She had already met Mum, who had come up to visit me in Leeds after I had told her all about Liz and she naturally wanted to meet the girl of my dreams, which went very well! We arrived in Suffolk the day before the wedding, where Liz got to know my Dad and meet my brother Richard, as well as Bill and Margaret Kelly with their family Dennis, Rita, Barbara and Diane. There's another book to be written!

It was a great wedding, though poor Mum got very drunk and was found in a ditch totally out of it. My Dad, who hardly ever drank, was furious! Liz recalls being cornered by my mother's sister Jean, who gave her the ultimatum that she must never hurt her favourite nephew, because she brought him up during the war, and this would be under the pain of death! Liz must have known then what she was letting herself into...

Liz's decision to move to London with me didn't go down well with her mother, so Liz invited me around to meet Mr and Mrs Rutherford, Doris and Wilson, to show that I was all right for their daughter. I totally understood and I'm sure that if I was a parent and my daughter wanted to leave home (which technically Liz had already done by being in Leeds for over a year) and then move in with a bloke she had met up there, then I probably wouldn't be overjoyed either. So I wanted to do my very best and not put a foot wrong...

I remember that before we were going to eat dinner, I suggested that I would go and get a bottle of wine for the occasion, as I had noticed there wasn't any in the house. Wilson said he would show me where the nearest off-licence was. I was grateful for his clever suggestion, as it meant that Liz and her mum could chat about me, while Wilson could get to know more about me. Wilson was a really lovely man, and very soon after we were married I would call him "Dad". Similarly, Doris became "Mum", which I know she was very happy about. I was very fortunate to have the best in-laws you could ever imagine.

Doris and Wilson were both from a town in the North East called Houghton-le-Spring. Amazingly, they didn't have a Geordie accent, unlike the rest of the family, who I got to know very well, though I often couldn't understand a word of what they were saying. Wilson had been an aircraft engineer, starting on busses in Sunderland and then coming down South to work for BOAC. His life's work really was studying every aircraft that came along, as he had to make sure it was fit for flying. In fact, he was responsible for signing out the Queen's flight, an unbelievably important job.

During the war, Wilson was asked to go out to Khartoum in Sudan, to be the engineer for BOAC flights that had to either pass though or stay there. Doris came out to join him, travelling via the Mediterranean on a troop ship, which must have been unbelievably dangerous, especially having to pass the Gibraltar Strait. She went as part of the Government's civil service, sorting passports and some apparently quite secret stuff, which I never did get out of her.

Now that I'd received the thumbs up from her parents, Liz was now safe to come and live with me. My next task was to find us somewhere to live. By coincidence, my mate Barry Halliday was also looking for a place, and his mother Dorrie knew of a ground floor flat in Sunningdale that was vacant. Apparently, it was a large three-storey manor house called Moorend, which had been converted and had unfurnished apartments on each floor, with at least half an acre of grounds. That sounded great! It got better when we found the cost of rent was just £14 per week. It might have been 1972, but this was still unbelievably cheap. The council rates were also £14, which meant between us the whole thing would cost £28! We rushed round to the estate agents, got a viewing and said yes immediately. The one proviso was that we had to keep the grass cut, though the owner, an Arab gentleman who lived in the country, would supply the equipment to mow the lawn. Perfect!

It was a fabulous apartment, with three large bedrooms, a kitchen, very large living room, bathroom and two toilets. The garden was a godsend, especially for an out-of-work actor. Barry and I made a mini golf course around the house. It even came with three garages, so I could park my Gilbern GT, Barry could park his Triumph Herald and we had one spare for visitors... All for £14 a week, it should have been at least three times that! Soon, Barry got a job working in the USA, teaching fight arranging. There he met an American girl, also called Liz, who was going to come back with him and live in the apartment with us, which meant we could now split the £28 four ways!

As you know, I occasionally filled in for Barry on fight arranging jobs while he was working in America. The strangest one was a play called *The Gentle Hook* by Francis Durbridge, a well-known crime thriller writer. The play had been on tour for about six weeks and was now coming to London's Piccadilly Theatre. I was asked to come to the final technical rehearsal before the opening and arrange the first scene where a lady returns home to find an intruder hiding behind a curtain. There is a scuffle and she stabs him to death. I was only given about half an hour to arrange this and I wondered why this hadn't been sorted out on tour? It turned out that Dinah Sheridan, who had been the leading lady stabbing the intruder on tour, was not doing the London run. The part was now going to be played by Hazel Bainbridge, who, with respect, was much older than Dinah. I was a little concerned that I had to arrange a fight scene with this petite actress in her sixties versus a 6'3" villain who must have weighed some 200 pounds.

The director was Basil Coleman, a well-respected purveyor of the theatre who knew exactly what he wanted. The man would approach an unsuspecting Hazel from behind. When he was to grab her, she had to throw him over her shoulder on to the settee, grab his knife and kill him. This of course is totally unbelievable, it could never happen, but I was there to arrange what Basil wanted and ensure that Hazel didn't hurt herself with the knife, which thankfully had been blunted.

After my half an hour was up, I was asked to stay on for the final dress rehearsal starting about 9pm. I of course agreed as they were paying me, but I realised I wouldn't be out of there before 1am, especially as I was told Basil would be giving notes after. I can't say I enjoyed the play, as I just couldn't believe that first scene. Anyway it came to the end and we were told to get a cup of whatever and come back for notes.

The notes started and I waited for Basil to give me hell over that totally dreadful and deeply unrealistic fight... nothing, not even a glare. Then came the best note I've ever heard, given to John Quinten, a lovely actor who was playing the detective sent to solve the crime. He was told by Basil, "John, on your first entrance through the double doors, as you walk down stage..." A long pause followed, then with passion Basil said "Act better!" Another long pause passed, before John, having thought it through and realised that this would likely be the best note he would ever receive, said "YES!" At this moment, I had to stuff my hanky in my mouth to stifle a laugh. Needless to say the play didn't last terribly long at the Piccadilly and thankfully I didn't get a credit in the programme!

I was grateful for this bit of pocket money from Barry though, as acting work was a little quiet on my return from Leeds. Though things were on the up for Liz, who joined the costume department at Thames Television. We also decided to adopt two cats, because a friend had kittens who needed a good home, which we were only happy to provide. We called these two tabbies Bilbo and Frodo. Despite being out of work, I was in a good place; I'd met the girl of my dreams, we had a great place to live and two lovely kittens. The icing on the cake would be if I could land myself a big role in a film, but that was never going to happen... was it?

CHAPTER 12

Let Me Tell You A Story

I was sat on my own in the flat at Sunningdale, wondering when my luck was going to change, when the phone rang. It was Hazel calling to say I had an interview for a feature film! I couldn't believe it. I was given all the details and later that week I arrived at an office in Hay Hill, Mayfair, where I was to meet Stephen Weeks, the writer and director. I was somewhat surprised to see that Ronald Lacey, an actor for whom I had an enormous respect, was also attending, but he was not there in his usual capacity, but as a production consultant for the film. Also present was Rupert Prior, one of the producers.

I was greeted with the feeling that they were glad to meet me, rather than the usual, "What have you done?" routine that actors become accustomed to in interview scenarios. I was told about the project, *Ghost Story*, which later became *Madhouse Mansion* in America; a terrible title, but it turned out there was already a film coming out over there with our title. The film would be shot in southern India, and I was invited to read the script to see if I liked it, as they were considering me for the part of Talbot. This had rarely happened to me and India was a country that I had never visited, but was definitely on my bucket list. I said I'd be delighted, and expected to be handed said script to take away and read... but no, I was asked to go to a room outside the office, take my time and come back when I was ready. Wow, this was definitely the first time this had ever happened in my career.

I left to read the script, though I must admit that I was feeling confused, it was all happening so fast. As I read, I saw the name Talbot appearing everywhere. I began to not take the storyline in, but kept thinking, "what do I say when I go back in there?" It was impossible for me to give any reasonable conclusion to my first reading, particularly as there obviously could be another actor waiting to be seen, so I thought I'd better get on with it. I have no idea how long I kept them waiting, but I went back in the room and was asked what I thought of the script, and from there all I can remember was being asked if I would like to do it. I was in a total daze. This was amazing; I had come from many an audition being told I had got the job, usually a commercial or mostly a play somewhere in the provinces, but never a major part in a feature film! Stephen Weeks later told me that he had enjoyed my performance in *Frontier* for the BBC and had wanted to cast me to play Talbot after his first choice, Malcolm McDowell, proved unavailable.

I left that office in Hay Hill with probably the biggest smile in London. I don't remember any of the journey home, though I do remember I didn't phone Hazel, as I wanted to let her tell me that I had been offered it (as if I didn't know). I knew I'd enjoy that. Sure enough, I got the call and all the details were confirmed. Not too long after, I had another meeting with Stephen, where we talked about practical things like the two C's; Costume and Character. There I discovered who else was in the film and was delighted to find out that Murray Melvin was part of the cast. Murray and I had of course worked together a few times before with Joan Littlewood at Stratford East, most memorably on *Oh, What a Lovely War*.

The next few weeks flew by; it felt like only days had passed since that first meeting. Before I knew it, I was waiting at Heathrow for the Air India flight to Bombay. Murray was there and I got introduced to Peter Hurst, our cameraman, and his assistant Jim Alloway. Next to arrive was actor Vivian MacKerrell, who as a drama student had shared a flat with future filmmaker Bruce Robinson, who would later use Vivian as the inspiration for Richard E. Grant's character in his film *Withnail & I*. Soon more of the cast arrived; Leigh Lawson, Anthony Bate, Barbara Shelley and Penelope Keith, whose career would be transformed just over a year later when she was cast as Margo Leadbetter in *The Good Life*.

We all boarded the long-haul Air India flight and, after ten hours or so, arrived at Delhi airport. I remember looking out of the window as we were landing and seeing families living at the side of the runway, they could only have been about twenty yards from the tarmac! We weren't allowed off the plane whilst it was picking up passengers for the onward flight to our next destination, Bombay. We were parked away from the terminal, but I was able to go to the open door where the steps were and was hit by the heat and smell of India and the many myna birds that were flying around the plane.

We eventually arrived in Bombay and after the obligatory check through Customs, we were met and taken to the house of an Indian actor/filmmaker, who I later found out had invested in the project. It had now been about 15 hours since we were assembled at Heathrow. I don't know about the others, but I was totally knackered and the journey wasn't even over yet, as we had hours to kill before our final flight to our destination, Bangalore. This house was next to a small harbour, where they were drying Bombay duck, a small fish that is popular in Indian restaurants. The smell was overpowering! We weren't given any time to look around though, as we were ushered inside to what appeared to be an anteroom, with plenty of chairs, but no real furniture. The owner wasn't at home, but we were offered tea and snacks and it was a chance to get to know our flying partners some more. We were all now very visibly tired and I think I dozed off for a bit whilst sitting up in a chair. Killing time is hard enough at the best of times, but doing so in a nice home that you weren't allowed to look around was a challenge. I think this part of the adventure lasted about six hours!

The journey finally continued and we eventually caught a short two-hour flight to Bangalore. After what seemed like an eternity to get through Customs, we were met by George Mills, our production manager, who had arranged two very nice Mercedes cars for us, complete with drivers (one of whom we nicknamed 'Two Planks': a nice lad, but 'thick as').

It was now time for another long journey, this time a three-hour drive up the mountains to Ootacamund, known as 'Ooty', where we were staying at the Maharaja of Mysore's Summer Palace. This would be a journey we would take a few times, as we had two main locations; one in Bangalore at another of the Maharaja's palaces, and the second in Ooty. It was a fascinating journey through the countryside of Tamal Nadu, driving through many villages, narrowly missing the cows who had right of way on the roads. We made one stop halfway to put water in the engine, which was overheating as we were going up and up. We were told not to get out of the car, as the local village children would likely ask us for gifts or money. We must have been there for ten minutes and did indeed attract a small crowd, mostly smiling children who looked as though they hadn't had a good meal in weeks. I made the fatal mistake of winding down my window and giving one child some rupee coins... All hell broke loose, the crowd suddenly doubled and dozens of children surrounded us, asking for money. Thankfully, 'Two Planks' finally come back with a watering can, filled the radiator up and off we went.

I seem to remember it was getting dark and eventually we came to the gates of our first home, where Stephen Weeks was waiting for us with a huge smile on his face, which I seem to remember was a permanent fixture. We were then introduced to Mr Das, our chef. He had a team of staff with him from Bangalore, who all stayed with us throughout the filming. I got to love these people, all of whom could not do enough for us. Mr Das had prepared some English food for us (where he got the beef from, we never asked!) After eating, I remember us all sitting in the drawing room, where we had a chat about the schedule. Sadly not all of the camera equipment had arrived and we would have to do what we could until it was released from Customs! The first day would therefore be an easy day. Thank heavens, I was totally knackered and couldn't wait to get to my room and sleep for as many hours as possible.

In the morning I could see Fernhill Palace in all its faded glory, it really was an ideal location for a film that was supposed to be set in England. Ooty is a hill station, some 8,000 feet up in the Nigiri Mountains. It was a place where the English Raj went to live out of the heat of Southern India. The palace, standing in its own grounds, was in need of a little, if not a lot, of TLC.

OH, WHAT A LOVELY MEMOIR

I suppose I should tell you what *Ghost Story* was about. Murray Melvin's character, McFadyen, had inherited this mansion, which of course was supposedly haunted. So he invites two friends from his university days to come and stay for a week, to see if this was really true. Except – spoiler – my character Talbot was not really a friend, he hardly knew him. He had also not been told about this ghost business. The other friend played by Vivian, called Duller, was fully aware and couldn't wait to get to work with an array of ghost hunting equipment. End of spoiler.

When filming on location, little problems often arise and of course we had already had our first, with parts of the camera equipment being held up in Customs, a persistent problem in certain countries. As we couldn't start work on the original schedule as planned, it was arranged to do a tracking scene featuring a Sunbeam-Talbot, a wonderful car borrowed from a local resident. We were to shoot the scene where Murray picks the two of us up from the station and drives us to his "strange inherited house". The crew, namely Jim Alloway, fixed the camera onto the bonnet and Murray and Vivian were positioned in the front, with me in the back. This gave the three of us a little time to rehearse with Stephen and get to know our characters and how we were going to develop them.

However, one large problem came with us using this wonderful Sunbeam-Talbot... it was an open-top car, so there was nowhere cameraman Peter Hurst could hold onto, let alone his focus puller or Jim Alloway. So the camera would have to roll without an operator. But what about sound? It was decided that our boom operator, a Mr Drampsey from our Indian crew, could be strapped to the running board of the car! So, with Murray driving, the three of us (and not forgetting Mr

Drampsey) went about half a mile away to our start point, leaving the rest of the crew, including the director, waiting for the result of our first take.

It was a quiet little road, just like a small Sussex South Downs road, with no houses or telegraph poles and hopefully no locals brewing tea on the side of the road. We got to our designated start point, where Jim Alloway was waiting for us to do the camera checks. As I was in the back, I was basically put in charge of the clapperboard, standing by to give "Action", while Jim was waiting to turn over the camera. We had a static rehearsal of the dialogue, which was very important to the story, as none of our characters really knew each other at university and only one, Murray's McFadyen, knew why he had invited the other two there… After our static rehearsal, we were ready to go. Jim put the camera to work, and we drove off. After a few seconds, I said the immortal words "Scene one, take one…" I slapped the clapper down and yelled "Action!"

We finished the scene and soon arrived back with the rest of the crew. Peter Hurst turned the camera off and Stephen Weeks asked us how it went. We were fairly happy, but thought we should do it a couple of times again, so that he ought to have at least one take that he liked. Stephen then asked Mr Drampsey how it went for him, as the only technician along for the ride. Mr Drampsey then responded with, "Ready when you are!" It turned out he hadn't actually recorded any sound during the first take, which was probably my fault because I should have said, "Turn over sound" before my "Action". Stephen decided that for the next take, he would be at the back, on the floor beneath me with my feet on top of him. That way, at least he could hear what we said and thump Mr Drampsey into action! I think we did two proper takes and then went off to continue doing as much as possible without our missing vital equipment.

I couldn't believe how small our crew was. Normally on location there would be enough people to fill Waterloo Station, but somehow it worked. Thankfully, the rest of the equipment arrived a couple of days later and Stephen could get back to his original schedule. Our second location in Bangalore was also a property of the Maharaja of Mysore; a real palace which was actually based on the living quarters of Windsor Castle. It had huge gardens, where a large troop of monkeys would enjoy trying to get into the palace at night. It took time to get used to their noise whilst trying to sleep!

We worked a six-day week and, as I was in almost every scene, I had very little time off to explore this amazing part of India. There are still some expats living in Ooty, which did have a strong feel of colonialism. We visited the Ooty Club a few times and when the shoot fell on my birthday, I invited the cast and crew there for a drink. Stupidly when I ordered a whisky, I had it with ice! The next day I was really suffering with a dodgy tummy and feeling sick. I had a scene with Murray where we were walking through the grounds. This took quite a time to organise, as it was a long tracking shot. At one point, I had to disappear to the bathroom, running ten minutes back to the palace. The shot was to finish with Murray and me walking past the camera. On the final take, I just made it in time before I threw up. When I look at that scene now, I can see myself fighting to control that eventuality! Though in hindsight, the look on my face was expressing exactly how my character was feeling at the time... maybe I was method acting?

In the palace, there was a room with a grand piano, where I liked to go after filming and play some jazz, not very well but it helped me unwind. An actor that hadn't yet joined us on location was Marianne Faithfull. When she arrived in Bangalore with her then boyfriend Oliver (who I got the impression only ever had one thing on his mind), Stephen brought Marianne into this room to meet me. I got up to say hello and shake her hand. She was wearing a very large picture hat, which covered her face unless she looked up. She asked who I was, and I told her my name was Larry and that I was playing the character Talbot. I don't think there was much of a response, and after they left, I continued playing the piano.

The next day we were shooting the first scene I had with Marianne, and the first thing she asked was who was I and which character was I playing? I of course gave her the same reply as I had the day before... Would you believe, this still happened once more? It was at this stage of her life that Marianne was sadly involved with taking drugs. Having said that, I thought she gave a super performance in the film and was very disciplined, even though she didn't know who I was.

The filming schedule was over six weeks, which might seem like a long time, but there was an awful lot to do. An added challenge was that we were filming in a large country with millions of people, none of whom could be shown in the background, as the script was set in an isolated English mansion. On one occasion whilst filming in the grounds of Bangalore, we were told of another film that was working about half a mile away from us. It was an Indian film, and a runner came over to us to ask if the star of our film could come over to meet the star of their film? It was agreed that I would go during our lunch break. When I got there, I announced myself and was told, "No we want to meet the star..." I suddenly got the point; the stars of Indian films are tall handsome men, with lots of makeup and an impressive moustache, and here was I; an average London boy, wearing drab clothes from the 1930s... I don't think I was the cinema idol they expected because they didn't bring their star out to meet me. So I walked back to our location, where we all had a good laugh about what happened.

I had a wonderful time making *Ghost Story*, I enjoyed the responsibility that I had never previously been given on a film and everyone was great to work with. I continued to see Murray over the years, usually at Stratford East events, though sadly I have hardly met any of the other cast or crew since. I certainly would have loved to see Vivian again, before his untimely death in 1995. Barbara Shelley came to our wedding and Penny Keith of course went on to become a huge star. One of the things that actors get used to is spending many good times working with a group of people and when filming wraps, you promise that you will all see each other again, but sadly in reality you rarely do.

Ghost Story is available on Blu-ray from Nucleus Films.

CHAPTER 13

Lady Luck

You need a lot of luck as an actor and in 1973, I'd already had my fair share. With that nice gig at Stratford, followed by six weeks making *Ghost Story* in India, it's fair to say that things were going well. Things change very fast in this game though, and now I couldn't get arrested as an actor! Liz was now settled into the Thames costume department, while Barry was back from the USA and getting plenty of work as a fight arranger in town. His new girlfriend from the USA, Liz Jamplis, was now living with us in the apartment at Moorend.

This was not a happy time for Liz Jamplis, living 30 miles out of London and not knowing a soul in Sunningdale. With Barry often working in town and my Liz down at Thames, she was stuck in the apartment all day, with only me for company; an out of work actor not knowing if he'd ever work again. She shut herself in their bedroom and wouldn't come out. I'd knock on her door and say, "I'm making a cup of tea Liz, would you like one?" There'd be a long pause... "No thanks". I'd then make my tea and go to the living room and put the telly on. Then as soon as I'd sat down, Liz would leave her room straight away, go to the kitchen and make the tea that she had said she didn't want, then go and shut herself back in her room again. This sort of thing happened all the time, and after a few weeks, the atmosphere at Moorend was getting terrible between the two of us. I confided to my Liz about this, but not Barry.

Liz and I had obviously saved a fair amount of money living at Moorend, thanks to the cheap rent. After a year, we decided it was time for us to apply for a mortgage and we agreed with Barry that we would be leaving once we had found a house to buy. Both sets of parents had promised us £2,000 each to go towards the £10,000 we needed for a deposit, meaning we'd just needed to save up £6,000 between us. However, getting a mortgage was much harder than I expected. Despite having savings with Halifax, they refused my application because I was an actor! Thankfully, Liz's contract at Thames meant that she could get a letter from her Head of Department, detailing what she would earn in a year. This helped us get a mortgage with the Property Owners' Association, at a half a percentage over the going rate. We took it and it was the best thing we could have done. Our friendships with Barry and Liz were saved and we were on the ladder.

Liz and I moved into our new home, a two-up two-down in Hanworth, with a long front garden and a back garden that backed onto the Hanworth Air Park, so named as that was where the airships left from. There was even room to park your car on the very wide pavement in front of the house. It was very exciting deciding how we were going to decorate and furnish, though quite difficult because at first we had little money to do anything. In fact, we didn't even have a penny left for a removal van, so my brother John kindly helped us on moving day in his Luton van. We couldn't even afford to buy food to feed our helpers, so our great friend Zelic made samosas for all to enjoy. Fortunately, I got some work and we bought some expensive Italian tiles for the bathroom, which I fitted with more care than you could possibly imagine. I am proud to say I didn't chip one! Aside from those tiles, cheap was definitely the word in the Dann household... except, it wasn't the Dann household yet, as I still hadn't popped the question...

It soon came to the point when Liz gave me the ultimatum... 'Marry me or I'm off' (well that's the way I saw it anyway). In fact, she was quite right as apart from it being the blooming obvious thing to do, our accountant advised that getting married halfway through a tax year would save us a fortune. So we decided to tie the knot. We met the curate at Ham Church, Mr Napley, and asked for permission to be married there. Liz made her own beautiful wedding dress and I went to Kings Road to buy a trendy suit. Liz also made all the invites, of which there were many, and we hired the Richmond Hill Hotel for the after party. Liz has always been a brilliant organiser, while I just sort of turn up! With all the hard work done, mostly by Liz, everything was ready for the day.

We got married on Saturday 6 October 1973, with Barry Halliday as my best man. Once again, all I had to do was turn up. We got to the church in plenty of time, and the weather was sunny and warm. As the guests started to arrive and wish me luck, I became nervous; not a thing that usually happens to me. The church was full and we stood awaiting the arrival of the bride, who would be walked down the aisle by her father Wilson, with her cousin Linda as her bridesmaid. The organ struck up with 'Here Comes the Bride' and as Liz stepped into the church, there was the loudest thunderclap and the heavens opened! Throughout the service, poor Mr. Napley was being drowned out by the sound of heavy rain falling on his church roof. I'm not sure I heard much of what he was saying to us.

It was soon time to walk down the aisle with my new bride and step out into the hell that had been made by the storm outside... but as we stepped out, the sun was shining and the ground was dry, extraordinary! We had our photos taken by the husband of one of Liz's school friends, who kindly did them as a wedding present. We then had a super reception, with plenty of food and booze laid on for our guests. I asked my friend Dave Gold, who was the musical director of *Forward Up Your End* when I was at E15, to provide a trio to play live music. Dave himself played the piano and after a few drinks, I ended up sitting beside him on stage and joining in on the old Joanna. Sorry Liz, you were now a Dann! Silly really, I should have taken on Rutherford, which is a much nicer name.

That night, we were going to Paris for our honeymoon, so we had to get home, change, pick up our luggage and then Barry kindly drove us to the airport to get on a late flight out of Heathrow. Just before the stroke of midnight, we arrived at our little hotel in Montmartre, cheap and cheerful. We arrived with only a few francs to spare, as we had spent too much on the wedding. But Paris was fantastic and we spent most days just wandering the streets, doing the usual sightseeing, including a visit to the Moulin Rouge. It got to the stage where Liz could either have a coffee or spend a penny, so we didn't go out for too many expensive meals. What a way to start our marriage!

LADY LUCK

Meanwhile back in Blighty, two new radio stations were just starting up, LBC and Capital Radio. On 8 October 1973 at 6.08am, I became the first commercial voice on LBC, narrating a commercial for Birds Eye Peas. Then on 16 October, I was the first voice in a commercial for Capital FM. Quite the claim to fame! I obviously never heard either of them, as Liz and I were still honeymooning. After we returned from our lovely time in Paris, I thought this might be the start of a new career. I did do a couple more of these voice jobs for the same company, but then I never heard a peep again.

However, I really did become the commercial king in the 1970s. I have absolutely no idea how many I was in, but it must have been dozens and dozens of them. I obviously had the right face at that time when they were looking for someone to play the average bloke or a gullible loser. It got to the point where I used to hear the other actors waiting to be auditioned saying, "Let's not bother, Larry's here!" They were very good earners too, as in those days on top of your basic fee, you also got residuals for every ten times the commercial was shown. This applied to all the regions too, so if you were lucky, you could be in a commercial that was showing in five different regions at the same time. It was of course impossible back then for the actor, or even the agent, to know where and when exactly these commercials were played, and so you had to rely on the honesty of the accountants from the various companies. The best one I did by far was for the Post Office, where my daily fee had been £250, though I eventually earned £15,000 in residuals from the showings! Ironically, I don't actually remember seeing this commercial, whereas others that I saw many a time only seemed to pay peanuts. Being greedy, those fees did not seem to relate to my Post Office one!

OH, WHAT A LOVELY MEMOIR

I was fortunate to work with some top directors on these commercials, including Alan Parker and Tony Scott. I also did four with his brother Ridley, though none of them ever called when they got to Hollywood! That looked set to change however, when I was cast in a Cadbury's Bar Six commercial, to be shot in Tangiers, Morocco and directed by Silvio Narrazino, a Canadian filmmaker with an Italian background, best known for directing the 1966 film *Georgy Girl*. I was told this commercial was going to be "the best one yet", and would be the first of six commercials in total, all shot in other parts of the world. The message being that you could get a Bar Six anywhere in the world. I was cast to star in all six, with the second one scheduled to be shot at the North Pole, followed by a Caribbean island for the third, and three more exciting destinations to follow. I was fitted out in a white tropical suit and off I went to Tangiers, to shoot in the Casbah for three days, alongside Milton Johns who had been cast as an 'Odd Job' character, spoofing the James Bond film *Goldfinger*. Also in the cast was a glamour model who had recently won a court case against a multi-millionaire, though at the final outcome she got a settlement of just 50p.

After arriving, we were put up in the lovely El Minzah hotel. Before we were to have dinner, Milton and I decided to have a look around the streets of Tangiers. This lasted about five minutes, because dozens of kids 'recognised' him as Odd Job, which of course he wasn't. So we made our escape back to the hotel! On arrival, Silvio invited me to join him in the bar for a drink, which of course I accepted. We were sat in these comfortable chairs, sipping our cocktails, when he said to me "I'm making a film and I'd like you to be in it." I obviously replied that I'd love that and asked him what the film would be about. He explained that it was not a big part, but the good news was he wanted me to play a policeman, who is picked up by a woman who is trying to make her husband jealous and she takes him to bed. He then adds, "This woman will be played by Brigitte Bardot..."

I couldn't believe my ears! There I was, sitting in a plush hotel in Morocco, having got a commercial to die for, being asked by the director to be in his next film, where I'd be working with the lust of my life. To say I was in heaven is an understatement! Naturally when I got back to England, I was telling anyone and everyone of my news. I was waiting for details about the next flight for my second Bar Six commercial when I got a call to say that Cadbury's had pulled the commercials. Then not long after that, the Bardot film was cancelled. Story of my life!

Another memorable commercial was when I was cast as a "handsome young man drinking coffee in a night club with a very glamorous woman." Very believable casting, wouldn't you say? Playing the glamorous woman opposite me was Vivien Neves, who at the time was possibly the most famous glamour model in the UK. She also happened to be the girlfriend of a London gangster, who provided a minder to be with Vivien while we were filming... perhaps worried that this "handsome young man" would whisk her away? We were shooting in one of London's famous nightspots, though we were filming in the daytime. Whilst we were waiting for things to start, which was usually most of the day with commercials, I started to chat to this minder, trying to find out what he actually did... He was quite open about his 'occupation' and I casually asked if he had ever killed anyone... straight away he said, "Yes". I took the courage to ask him what happened...

He said coldly "I ran him over with a van." Not being able to even imagine taking someone's life, I asked him, "What did you feel?" He replied, after a long pause… "Bump". Feeling a shiver, I drank my coffee. Needless to say, I didn't try to chat up Miss Neves!

Aside from the odd conversation with a ruthless killer, I enjoyed my commercial life. I had some lovely jobs overseas, with Holland being particularly good to me. In fact, I once made a commercial in Amsterdam for one company, came home and then the next day I travelled back to Amsterdam to do another one for a different company. Why? Because the two companies wouldn't agree on who would pay for an overnight stay, and so they ended up spending more on two separate airfares! The way those companies used to spend money on these commercials was unbelievable. I once enjoyed a week in Tenerife making a holiday commercial with lovely Lesley Duff, to be one of many shown at Christmas time. We only filmed on the last day, having been told to spend the previous six days getting a suntan… I've never worked so hard in my life!

Of course, 'Lady Luck' is not always on your side when dealing with these huge companies… I made two television commercials for Armstrong Rhino Floor, which were good fun to make as I was being chased by a magnificently made life-size rhino model. So far, so good. But months later, Liz got a call from her cousin Linda up in Durham, saying that she'd seen a large cut-out poster of me in a shop, advertising Armstrong Rhino Floor… I had no idea about this! Apparently these cut-outs of me were in DIY stores all over the north of England and they had never agreed a fee with me. I suppose they'd thought that as I was unlikely to ever see them, they'd

LADY LUCK

see if they could get away with it... I contacted Hazel and a fee was agreed.

On another occasion, I had been cast as the new milkman for the Milk Marketing Board. This was a good gig to get, as these famous adverts dated back to the 1950s and I had been offered a year's contract. I went to have some photos taken of me dressed in my milkman's gear, which I assumed were internal costume pictures. After waiting to find out my filming days, I was told that after many years, these famous commercials would not be made anymore... Just my luck! As we hadn't filmed anything yet, the contract could be cancelled without them having to pay me. Never mind, I was doing well from commercials as a whole and the money was providing some security and allowing me to be able to do more theatre work, which was my first love.

About a month later, I was driving into town and saw this giant poster at the junction of Earls Court. It was me, holding a couple of bottles of milk, wearing the uniform from that photo shoot. Unbelievable! They had cut the contract, not paid me for the photo shoot, then plastered my face all over Earls Court. Then of course, as I continued my drive into town, all I can see is this damn poster everywhere! That night, I even saw it on an episode of *Sykes* with Eric Sykes and Hattie Jacques. Once again, I got on the phone to Hazel, who came back to say that she had got me a fee for the photo shoot, but nothing for the posters, as she didn't want to upset the commercial agency... The fee she had agreed for me was £30! This was the final straw and after 25 years I decided it was time to look for a new agent. More on that later...

I think I can also claim a record for the most takes of a single shot in a commercial. This was for Esso Petrol, who at the time were advertising a scheme where for every four gallons of petrol you bought, you would get vouchers for a free drinking glass. For the commercial, I was sat on a stool in a little studio in High Street Kensington, with a hand artist just off-camera, who would pass me a glass to drink various concoctions from, showing off the versatility of the product. I think there were a total of five drinks, including orange juice, milk, whisky, and heaven knows what else, anything they could put in a glass… Now imagine a close up of my face, with a hand coming in and giving me this glass to drink from, five times. Each time, I had to show delight at this amazing glass, and all this had to be within 25 seconds, leaving the other five seconds for the product caption…

We started and after about five takes, the director was concerned that the hand artist wasn't getting the glass perfectly in frame, which was admittedly a very hard thing to do in such a tight close up. The glass had to come to a precise point within a few millimetres, making sure not to cover my face, whilst also showing the glass from the best perspective – all while not spilling any of the contents. We went again and again, until after about fifteen takes, the hand artist's hand was understandably starting to shake. We stopped for a while to give him some time to relax. I then noticed a row of men in suits sitting against the back wall. I wondered if these were executives from Esso? I was right.

Our director was now going over to talk to them, which seemed to be happening after every shot. After about the thirtieth take, having held approximately 150 glasses of fluid in front of my face, the hand artist had to be given his cards, as he was now having a breakdown. Poor sod, the job he had been given was almost impossible. More discussions followed with the suits and it was finally agreed with the cameraman (the super Derek Vanlint, who I seemed to work with a lot) that we would move to a wider shot and not be so close to my face, so as to give the hand more of a chance of getting it right...

As for me, having done at least thirty takes of drinking a combination of coloured water, milk and orange juice, I was now feeling a little bloated. I did have a bucket beside me, to spit out whatever remained in my mouth when "Cut" was called. But now there was no hand artist on set, so the first assistant said he would do it. He was duly sent off to makeup for a manicure! While this was happening, Derek quietly told me that he had got the shot on take five! He also told me that this was the director's first time making a commercial. Take 50 came and a polite round of sarcastic applause went around the room... though the suits didn't join in! I was now only thinking of the money that I might make from this ridiculous situation. The madness continued and take 100 arrived! By now the atmosphere was not good, especially from me. I remember saying that I would have to go to the toilet, as I was feeling sick, which was the only thing I could think of, not only to get out of the studio for a while, but hopefully for the suits and the director to come to their senses and call it a day...

No such luck. I like to think of myself as a professional who will always do his best to help make a job as good as it can be, but by this point, I was really not feeling very well. They decided to break for lunch! They took me to this restaurant, but I was so bloated I was barely able to eat anything. We went back to the studio and eventually got to, hand on heart, take 150! Same close up, same glasses of liquid, same chatting to all the suits after each take. I finally stood up and said, as calmly as I could, "Goodbye, I'm going home". I went to the dressing room, collected my belongings and walked out. No one tried to stop me. There was a phone box outside the studio. I phoned my new agent and explained what had happened, so as to cover myself in case of repercussions. We never heard a word from the company. They paid the fee, though as far as I know, the commercial was never shown, as I never saw any repeats. A few years later, I went to another commercial casting. I entered the room and couldn't believe it when that very same director greeted me with "Nice to see you again!" I phoned my agent and I said, "If they want to cast me for this one, tell them I'm busy."

Just Married! Family and friends join us for our special day.
(Author's Collection)

CHAPTER 14

Carrying On

For every actor, there is many a time when things don't go your way. Missed opportunities? I've had my fair share. Most of them weren't going to change my life, but there were a few that might have done...

As a twelve-year-old, when I didn't know what it meant to be given a "nice part", I was cast in the Norman Wisdom film *Trouble in Store*. I had a character name, which I can't remember now, but I do recall arriving for my first day of filming in Brighton, only to be told that my part had been given to another boy, who was also from Corona and had been supplied by Hazel Malone for the filming. I later got the impression that this other boy was a favourite of Hazel's and that she wanted him to have the part. There was a lot of that going on at the time and it took me a while to get on Hazel's favourites list. At the time, it didn't bother me. In fact, I didn't even tell my Mum what had happened.

But looking back on my career in this crazy business now, it is the feature films that got away which hurt the most. For example, in 1968 I was cast in the film *Performance* where I was going to play Mick Jagger's friend. I couldn't wait to start, but in the end I didn't start at all, as the part was cut from the film during pre-production. The following year, the same thing happened to me on the film *Loot*, where I was cast to play a detective constable to Richard Attenborough's Inspector Truscott. Hazel had agreed a fee, but the part was then cut before filming, apparently for cost reasons... as I hadn't yet signed a contract, guess how much I got? *Loot* was directed by Silvio Narizzano, who later let me down on the Brigitte Bardot film. Perhaps he was trying to tell me something?

But as a jobbing actor, you have to roll with the punches and I have also had plenty of luck along the way. I have appeared in dozens of feature films and, perhaps most memorably, I was very fortunate to be in four of the iconic *Carry On* movies. My first was *Carry On Teacher* back in 1959 when I was 18 years old, far too old to be playing a secondary school kid! When I turned up at Pinewood for a day's filming, I thought I would just be filling in a space in the classroom. I hadn't seen a script or even met the director, Gerry Thomas. Imagine my surprise when I was chosen to be the lad who put his hand up, wanting to be excused to go to the loo!

The concept of the *Carry On* films was very new. *Carry on Teacher* was the third one to be made and I hadn't seen the first two, *Carry on Sergeant* and *Carry on Nurse,* so I was totally unaware of who all these actors were. For me it was just fun being on set with lots of my Corona mates, including Richard O'Sullivan, Roy Hines, Paul Cole, George Howell and Carol White. There were many others I could name but it could take up twenty pages and I would be certain to forget someone and be cursed for the rest of my life!

I remember doing this little scene and getting a laugh from the crew as I exited from the classroom and Gerry said, "Cut". "Happy with that", I thought to myself and, as they didn't do another take on it, I was feeling really good. Most times you would be asked to do at least four takes, so that the director and his editor could chose the best one, not only for the performance, but the overall look of the shot. Well, the whole scene, which featured Kenneth Connor as our teacher Mr Adams, Leslie Phillips and Rosalind Knight as the inspectors, and of course the great Ted Ray as the headmaster, only took about two hours to complete. I began to be aware that they didn't hang about here, obviously something I would have to get used to in later years. I have done scenes in films that have sometimes taken days to complete and these weren't complicated ones with plenty of action or movement either.

At the end of that day on *Carry on Teacher*, I got my cards and climbed back on the coach that had taken us all from Chiswick to Pinewood and thought no more about it. A few days later, Hazel phoned to say that they wanted me to do another scene, this time playing in an orchestra. I had really enjoyed my first day, so off I went again. Brilliant! This time the scene was set in the school hall, where the pupils were performing the end of term play, Shakespeare's *Romeo And Juliet*. Charles Hawtrey played the conductor Mr Bean (not that one!) I was to be in the orchestra playing the timpani, those huge drums that look like a witch's cauldron.

Now, this scene took a lot of setting up and if you've seen the film, you can see why. There was so much calamitous action, which took a lot of clearing up if we had to do a retake. Part of the calamity was caused when the orchestra decided we were fed up of playing the dirge that Charles Hawtrey's character had written, so we went and played jazz instead. I was given a moment to perform a jazz drum solo that ended up in total chaos, with sticks and drums flying everywhere. I don't usually blow my own trumpet, but when I finished I got a round of applause from the crew and a few of my Corona mates. Even the legendary Leslie Phillips came up and congratulated me! The first and last time that has happened to me on a film set. So you can imagine my disappointment when I went to see *Carry on Teacher* and discovered that this part of the scene had been cut from the film. My best bit!

It wasn't until 1975 that I would step back into the franchise, which by this time had become hugely successful, totalling 26 feature films and a series of television specials. I had an audition with Gerry Thomas for a commercial, which he said I wasn't right for, but he said he would like me to be in his next *Carry On* film. As an actor, you often hear things like this that come to nothing, but Gerry was true to his word and not long after that I was cast in *Carry On Behind*.

The premise of this one was that a Roman burial site was suspected to be buried beneath a caravan site. Therefore you had the jolly campers being disrupted by the archaeologists carrying out their research. Kenneth Williams starred as Professor Crump and Elke Sommer played Anna Vrooshka the Roman expert. I was to play Clive, one of their archaeology students, alongside Brian Osborne as Bob.

The location selected for the Riverside caravan site was the back lot at Pinewood. This was only to be a four week shoot, as producer Peter Rogers never liked his films to take much more than that, hence why we always had to try and get each shot done in no more than two takes! The main problem with the schedule was that we were filming in March and it was supposed to be mid-summer! It was blooming cold and often wet, and our characters were of course dressed in light clothing and swimwear. The other problem for the crew was that being springtime, there were hardly any leaves on the trees and with the rain, the ground was becoming very muddy. In the end, the production team employed an old trick they had first used on *Carry on Camping*: the mud was painted green and false leaves were stuck to the trees! Fortunately, Mr Rogers had allowed a few caravans to be placed nearby, for the cast to use to stay out of the cold… his generosity knew no bounds! These problems forced the schedule to be extended, which meant I was paid twice my fee, though that was still not very much.

This being my first *Carry On* where I was on contract for every day, I got to know the legendary cast and we had many a laugh. I was fortunate to share a lot of scenes with Kenneth Williams, who was very friendly and full of stories; similar to how he appeared on his famous TV interviews, though not as camp. He was a different person off camera. I can say that Kenneth couldn't stand Elke Sommer, he told me that her breath smelled dreadfully and that she suffered with B.O. It could be that Kenneth had found out that Elke was being paid a lot more than him, reportedly six times his salary! I have to say that Elke didn't fit the company feel; she would hardly say a word to anyone.

I loved the moments in between takes when we sat relaxing in our caravan and chatting to, or mostly listening in awe of, the two Kenneths, Bernie Bresslaw, Windsor Davies, Peter Butterworth, Ian Lavender, Liz Fraser, Jack Douglas and the two young actresses that Brian and I were lucky to be teamed up with: Carol Hawkins and Sherrie Hewson. It felt great being accepted by all those superb comic actors.

The following year, I was thrilled to be asked back, this time for *Carry On England*, which was set in a training camp for squaddies during the Second World War. Once again we were on the back lot at Pinewood, where we shot lots of scenes of the boys and girls getting up to no good, with poor Kenneth Connor as our Captain constantly losing all control of his platoon.

I remember we shot one scene set in an underground bunker actually made out of tons of Fuller's earth, which made it much easier for the crew to clear away after we finished. As I wore a wedding ring, I was asked to take it off for filming, something I have had to do many times when playing a single man. When we finished for the day, I went to my pocket and discovered my ring was missing! I went straight back to the set and told the scene boys what had happened. They told me not to worry and that they would sift through all the Fuller's earth and find it for me… I went home and didn't tell Liz what had happened, hoping that the boys would find the lost ring.

The following morning, I got in the car to drive to Pinewood and lo and behold, there was my ring on the floor next to the brake pedal! I had no idea how it got there, I was convinced I had taken it off in the dressing room and put it in my costume pocket. I got to the studio and the boys, who had spent hours searching for my ring, felt dreadful that they hadn't found it. I had to come clean and tell them I had found it. I was very apologetic, but I think they forgave me because they had got some overtime for the search.

We had many laughs on *Carry On England* and director Gerry Thomas encouraged fun at all times, except when the camera was running. He wanted no corpsing, in other words no laughing during a take. I had this scene with Kenny Connor where he, as Captain S. Melly, had a moustache and a twitch and I, as Gunner Shaw, had exactly the same. During inspection, Kenny comes to me and says, "Stop twitching" to which I say, "I'm not twitching, you are" and it goes on with both of us twitching and denying it. I can honestly say that, to me, Kenneth Connor was the funniest of comedic actors and, of course, I kept corpsing. After about four takes, Gerry shouted, "CUT!" and had to get angry with us. I blame Kenny, because he had that twinkle in his eye that would set you off and I know he was doing it on purpose! We did get it right a couple of takes later. I'm sure when Peter Rogers found out that we had done six takes on a shot, his wallet must have had a seizure!

It was during *Carry On England* that I was also working in the West End on a rock musical called *Leave Him To Heaven*. It starred Brian Protheroe and featured a young Anita Dobson, later to find fame as Angie Watts in *EastEnders* and marry Queen guitarist Brian May. I had been given permission to leave Pinewood by 5:30pm each night, so I could get to the New London Theatre in time for the 8pm curtain rise. We also performed a matinee at 5pm on a Friday. I did get very tired, not because of the work, but the travelling from home to Pinewood and then on to the West End and then hopefully home by midnight. I did this for four weeks and eventually got laryngitis, which meant I really struggled with my so-called singing voice! Fortunately it didn't interfere with the few lines I had in *Carry On England*, as if it had, Mr Rogers would have had to pay for me to go to the dubbing theatre to re-record them. I would have really been in his good books then! But as a whole, I had a great time filming and was getting used to being a small part of the *Carry On* team.

OH, WHAT A LOVELY MEMOIR

And now we come to 1978 and once again I got a call from my agent, telling me that they would like me to be in the next one, *Carry On Emmannuelle*. I thought, "Wow, that would be great!" I knew I wouldn't make much money again, but what fun it would be to be back working with the same crew. Of course, I said yes and waited for the details. I think it was the next day when my agent called again to say that they would be sending me a script and that it would be another four week schedule, but this time I would be paid £4,000, a lot of money in those days! I hasten to add that none of the cast ever got residuals, and when you think how many times they have been shown on TV or released on video and DVD, not one penny of those sales has gone to the actors... Mr Rogers knew what he was doing and it's no wonder he was not respected.

The script duly arrived and I started to read it, looking forward to discovering how much my character, Theodore Valentine, had been given to do. The very first scene was set on Concorde, where the titular Emmannuelle, played by Suzanne Danielle, was sitting opposite Theodore, scantily dressed. A steward offers Emmannuelle some champagne, to which she doesn't respond. He then asks, "Is there anything Madame would like?" At which point, Emmannuelle was scripted to smile and undo his zipper, then passenger calls out, "Steward, are you coming?" I can't tell you how disappointed I was; first page and basically smut. It was awful and, of course, it got worse. I couldn't believe Gerry Thomas wanted this type of blatant humour instead of the usual cheeky seaside postcard fun. I began to understand that the *Carry On* team felt that they had to compete with the successful *Confessions* films starring Robin Asquith, but surely not this way? I didn't know what to do. Did I call my agent to say how unhappy I was, especially as I had to be in many more unfunny scenes?

Fortunately, I soon received a revised script, which was still over the top, but hopefully we could manage to make it work as a *Carry On*... I then got a call from Courtenay Elliott, the costume designer, wanting to take me out to buy all my costumes, which was a first for me on a *Carry On*. Once we had all my suits, jackets and trousers, I was ready for my first day's filming. As is usual on films, you rarely shoot scenes in story order, and my first scene scheduled for filming was at the Embassy, where Emmannuelle lived with her husband Emile, played by Kenneth Williams. Theodore was arriving to meet her for the first time after the cavorting on Concorde, which had yet to be shot.

The scene was set in the bedroom, where Emmannuelle was on a sun bed and Kenneth's character was leaving to go to a meeting. Whilst Suzanne and Kenneth were doing the first part of the scene, I waited backstage, amazingly with the producer Peter Rogers. Peter, who over the years had never said a word to me, was there to introduce me to Suzanne. It seemed like we were waiting for quite a while, as true to form he didn't say a word to me. Thankfully, Suzanne eventually came off the set, followed by director Gerry Thomas, who explained what we were going to do in our scene.

We went on set for a rehearsal, where I saw the sun bed for the first time. Suzanne was to be lying face down, naked on the bed. I was then to enter and, embarrassed to see her naked, walk backwards and do a little trip up some steps and fall on her, with my hand landing on her bottom. Once we were ready for a take, the set became closed, which meant anyone not immediately involved with the scene had to leave the studio, as Suzanne would be naked. I remember feeling nervous, waiting outside the door I was to enter through. "Action" is called and I enter, start the dialogue and come to the point where I trip, but as we hadn't rehearsed the practicalities I ended up missing putting my hand on her bum and my face landed there instead. I apologised and said, "Nice to meet you, Suzanne", which got a good laugh and Gerry said we had better have another go. I have to say, Suzanne was very brave with not only the way she handled this scene, but the many more like this she had to do in the film.

My first day came to an end and I began to realise that this film would not be as much fun to make as the previous ones. Although the cast and crew were just as great as before, there was an atmosphere of disappointment. I know Kenneth Williams was very unhappy that he did *Emmannuelle*. We had many a chat about almost everything, he was very interested in history and could be bitchy about so many people (no names, no pack drill... whatever that means?) But we didn't have the same number of laughs or banter that we had shared together before, which was a great shame.

On a happier note, a highlight for me was working with Beryl Reid, who was wonderful to me. She obviously didn't know me from Adam, but she was so generous as an actress that she gave me an awful lot to play off. We originally only had one scene together, where Beryl was playing Theodore's Mum. Gerry liked how we bounced off each other so much that he had another scene written, the one where Theodore tries to shoot himself. It was a privilege to have worked with Beryl.

CARRYING ON

In the old days when I first started, I used to eat in the canteen, but now as a proper cast member I could use the Pinewood restaurant, where I would usually sit with another member of the *Carry On* team. On one occasion I was on my own and a man I hadn't seen before asked if he could join me. He was obviously an American by his accent and he asked me what I was working on. I explained and in turn I asked him who he was. He said he was also an actor and was over in the UK for several months filming the first *Superman* movie... He introduced himself as Christopher Reeve! I then became rather starstruck, as I had heard about him. We didn't really talk about films after that, but more generally about life and probably the weather. After half an hour, I had to get back on set and we said our goodbyes. I kept going back to that restaurant, but we never met again. At least for that one day, I got to have lunch with Superman!

When you are in a film and have a reasonable part, you usually get invited to a screening. I awaited this invitation, but it never arrived. Eventually I noticed *Carry On Emmannuelle* was opening at a cinema in Clapham Junction. Liz and I decided to go to an afternoon show and we got seats in the front row of the circle. There was hardly anyone there, just a few fans sitting at the back. I was extremely nervous as to what I was about to see, especially as Liz was with me! The film started with the Concorde scene and at the end it got a good laugh from the fans at the back. That was possibly the last laugh I heard. The film finished and I felt totally embarrassed at what I had witnessed. Not wanting anyone to recognise me, we got up to leave and noticed that the fans in the back row had already gone and the circle was empty, devoid of all life. Downstairs was similarly barren. Thank heavens!

Over the years, I have been to a few *Carry On* events, where the fans are amazing and always very complimentary... except about *Carry On Emmannuelle*.

Recording the *Carry On Teacher* DVD commentary with Paul Cole, Richard O'Sullivan and comedy historian Robert Ross. We had many a laugh! *(Courtesy of Robert Ross)*

Left: Comedy policeman for hire. Right: With my dear friend Melody Kaye in *The Plotters of Cabbage Patch Corner* at the Shaw theatre. *(Author's Collection)*

Corona reunion. Opposite me is Rona Knight, who I have an awful lot to thank for. At the far end is Hazel Malone, my agent for 25 years. *(Author's Collection)*

Backstage at the Leeds Playhouse, my Mum came up to visit and meet Liz, who can be seen giggling in the background. *(Author's Collection)*

Our wedding day, 6th October 1973! (L-R) Liz's parents Wilson and Doris Rutherford, the happy couple, my Mum and Dad. *(Author's Collection)*

More wedding day snaps. Bottom left: my Best Man Barry Halliday. Bottom right: Liz and I play the piano at our reception before going to Paris that night. *(Author's Collection)*

Relaxing with our wonderful pets, Gimli the dog and Bilbo the cat. They slept with me many times like that. *(Author's Collection)*

Posing in 2023 with my original 1991 TV Times magazine, where I appeared on the cover with my *The Bill* co-stars Trudie Goodwin and Jon Iles. *(Author's Collection)*

Supporting a charity event for the Metropolitan Police with my *The Bill* co-stars (L-R) Roger Leach, Robert Hudson and Colin Blumenau. *(Author's Collection)*

The Bill cast supporting *Children In Need* in 1989. *(Courtesy of Paul Jackson)*

Playing a charity football match at Wembley with members of the *Coronation Street* and *EastEnders* casts for *Children In Need* 1991. *(Author's Collection)*

Trudie Goodwin and Andrew Mackintosh present me with the Sierra Oscar award for 'Best Comedy Performance in a Police Series' at a Christmas party. *(Author's Collection)*

Left: Z-Lister doing the panto circuit. *(Author's Collection)* Right: Falling back in love with the theatre in *The Jests of Skoggan* in 2000. *(Courtesy of Steve Morley)*

Howzat! Still keeping fit in my 80s. *(Courtesy of Chadwick Cricket Club)*

With my Walking Football teammates in Portugal, 2016. *(Courtesy of Mark Blythe)*

Liz and I celebrated our Golden Wedding Anniversary in 2023. *(Author's Collection)*

CHAPTER 15
Brushes With The Law

I had spent the first three decades of my career playing characters on the wrong side, whenever the law was concerned. My dealings with the police in real life had been limited to two horrific traffic accidents I witnessed, both of which still haunt me to this day. The first was in the 1960s when I was on my way to a Bonfire Night party. I was driving behind a van that hit a pedestrian on Ham Parade. The poor man flew through the air like a rag doll and landed beside my car. I got out and shouted out for someone to call an ambulance. Both the man's legs were broken and he was shaking. I cradled him, then suddenly a voice screamed, "That's my husband!" and a woman came running over and threw herself on us both. After what seemed like an eternity, the ambulance arrived but by then it was too late, the man had died in my arms. By the time the police took my statement, I was suffering from shock, but unbelievably I was allowed to drive myself home!

Then one year in the 1970s on Christmas Eve, I was travelling back from Stratford East to Hanworth at night. Passing the Twickenham Rugby roundabout, a Mercedes flew past me at ridiculous speed. Within seconds, I could see an old gentleman standing in the road about 100 yards away, waving his arms at me. I stopped and couldn't believe what I saw. The Merc was upside down on its roof, totally crushed flat with the wheels still turning. I stopped and thought what if the driver was still in there? I ran over and got on my knees to look inside, but there was no one in there. I looked around for a body while the gentleman was still waving in shock. Then at least fifty yards ahead, I saw the engine had landed in the centre of the road and then another twenty yards away was the body. His trousers had come off and were hanging on his ankles, making his legs look twice as long. There was a little blood coming out of one ear, and his arms were by his side as if at attention. It was an unbelievable sight. He had apparently hit the iron pedestrian bridge whilst swerving to get around the waving gentleman. What speed must he have been doing? Strangely, I felt more sorry for the waving gentleman; what must he have seen, the horror of that crash. I hoped he didn't blame himself for what had happened. I never got to speak to him or offer my support, as soon a police car arrived and after establishing that I hadn't witnessed the crash, this officious constable basically told me to piss off. Neither harrowing experience left me holding the police in especially high regard.

It wasn't until 1981 that I would play my first copper. I was cast by director Don Taylor in a new television series for the BBC called *Maybury*, a 'case of the week' medical drama starring Patrick Stewart. I was told that, even though I would only be in one episode, my character of PC Adam was a good part and "very integral to the plot". There would be one day's location filming, then four weeks off before the studio scenes would be recorded. In turn, I would be paid a wage to keep me available and prevent me from taking any other work that would interfere with their studio schedule. This was brilliant because Liz and I had been planning a trip to the USA, including her first visit to New York, where we were going to see our best man Barry Halliday. We were then going over to LA to visit Barry's ex-wife, Liz Jamplis. This four-week break in the schedule on the *Maybury* gig would be ideal for our trip!

It was soon time for me to do my single day of location filming. I was called to the famous BBC Television Centre in White City for 7am, where I went to meet the costume designer, who had previously taken my measurements on the phone. I was put into my police uniform, which thankfully fitted perfectly, and within half an hour I was in reception waiting for a car to take me to the location, which was a small car park by Lambeth Bridge. All sounds straightforward enough? Except that, even up to that moment of being taken to location, I have still not received a script and have literally no idea of what I am about to be doing! During the journey, I ask the lady from wardrobe who is accompanying me whether she knows what we are going to be filming. She informs me that PC Adam will be seen crossing Westminster Bridge, when he hears a large explosion on the river next to the Houses of Parliament. Apparently Kenneth Haigh's character is responsible and I am going to arrest him! Well at least now I know what's happening.

We arrived at the car park, where there was a coach for everyone not yet required on set to sit on. I also spotted a caterer, who I hoped was getting the bacon sandwiches ready! I got on the coach, and found Kenneth Haigh was already there. I introduced myself and we had a little chat, the usual, "nice to meet you, thank heavens it's not raining" sort of small talk. Mr Haigh had been lucky enough to be given a script, so whilst he carried on studying it, I grabbed a bacon sandwich, found myself a seat and waited for instructions. I was also hoping to meet Don Taylor, who I hadn't worked with before.

OH, WHAT A LOVELY MEMOIR

Fortunately, I had brought some reading matter with me and so the first couple of hours, during which time Kenneth Haigh was called to set, passed fairly quickly. Just before lunch, an assistant director climbed on the coach to tell me that I should be used after lunch. I asked if I could have a copy of the script and was informed I would get one later. I'm now finding this all very strange... PC Adam is apparently "very integral to the plot", but I've still not been given a script? Hours go by and eventually at about 5pm, I am called to the 'set'. I was taken to Westminster Bridge, where at last I met Don Taylor, who explained that he wanted me to be walking over the bridge, hear a big bang to my right over the river, then run out of shot. "No problem." We did this a couple of times with a few extras playing civilians, who also had to react to the soundless bomb! "Cut!" I was then sent back to the coach with all the extras.

During all the time on the coach, I had been planning our trip to America. My idea was that early the next morning, I would go to Victoria, pop into the Freddie Laker offices and book our flight to New York. At the time, Laker offered unbelievably cheap daily flights to NY for just £50 on a first come, first served basis. No frills, but you could bring your own sandwiches and drink on board. Imagine that now?

But back on the coach, I was beginning to panic, as I knew I still had to do a shot running down the steps opposite the Houses of Parliament and arrest Mr Haigh. There could have only been an hour of daylight left to get this done and I was worried that they might call me back to do this shot tomorrow. Fortunately after a few minutes, I was called back onto 'set'. Don Taylor said that, considering the time we had left, he would take for granted that I had run down the steps, and that they would start the shot at the bottom of the steps, with

Kenneth pulling in on his little boat. I would then move in and make the arrest.

So, there I am with my back to camera whilst the shot was being lined up. The cameraman then started moving me about, casting a shadow from the lowering sun, which was going down behind Parliament. I was now aware that I was being used as what is known in the business as a 'French Flag', stopping sun flare on the camera lens. We went for a rehearsal, "Action" was called and the little boat started coming towards me, starting possibly fifty yards away from me. As the boat got nearer, the cameraman was adjusting my shoulder to help with the shadow and prevent lens flare. The boat got to about five yards away, when suddenly the skipper turned the boat back out into the river. "CUT!" screamed Don, quickly followed by "What the fuck are you doing?" The skipper told him that it was too shallow for the boat to get any closer. Don yelled, "We must get this shot. Go back and do it again!"

We reset and "Action" is called. This time, the boat got a little closer, but once again it veered away... Well, Don Taylor really lost his rag, like all hell had broken loose along the Thames. He reluctantly made the decision to scrap the scene. I was taken back to the coach and told "We'll see you in four weeks when we do the studio." I asked if a script could be sent to me, then went back to the BBC, got changed and drove home to Liz. We decided we would try for a flight tomorrow morning. By this time, I was being represented by a new agent, who, for reasons which will become clear later on, I shall refer to in this book as Agent X. I phoned Agent X to explain our vacation plans, but they told me that I really wasn't allowed to leave the country, as per my contract. I said that I would take the chance, especially as they had only used me as a French Flag!

OH, WHAT A LOVELY MEMOIR

Early next morning, I got to Freddie Laker at Victoria and booked two one-way tickets to New York, leaving that day, plus two onward tickets to Los Angeles. Success! We were only going to be in NY for one week, but that was enough time to show Liz all the sights. We met up with Barry Halliday, who was letting us stay in a flat on 2nd Avenue that he shared with a mate, who happened to be away. It was on the top floor of a four-storey house. Getting into it was like accessing Fort Knox; not only the front door, but the door into the flat, which had at least four keys, one of which released an iron bar that jammed the door from being barged open. I remember the biggest problem with this was whenever we got back during the daytime and needing a pee, panic would often set in as it sometimes took us ages to get the blooming place open! I have to say that this wouldn't have been our holiday flat by choice, but it was free, and in the basement of this house was a bar, which was open all hours. We didn't know this at first.

Basically we had one room with a bed and small kitchen. The bathroom had a skylight window, which was protected by barbed wire. No bugger was getting in this place! That first night, when we got into bed, there was a lot of noise coming from the bar below. I put the light on to have a look and suddenly what seemed like hundreds of cockroaches made for cover! I remembered that spectacle from my first time in NY and I'll never forget that noise, you didn't want to put your feet on the ground. Anyway, once the roach army had disappeared, we went to the window looking out onto the street to see dozens of people having a disagreement, mostly with their fists.

We watched for a while, then the sounds of police sirens followed. Just like the cockroaches before them, the participants of this foray into street violence rapidly disappeared, just before four or five police cars arrived on the scene. The police officers did their routine of going into the bar, looking down the road, scratching their bits, looking tough, before getting back into their squad cars and driving off into the night, having not arrested a soul. Within a minute of their departure, the vanishing troublemakers were back, though now they all seemed to be the best of friends and went into the bar for another drink! It must have now been 2am. What entertainment we had on our first night on 2nd Avenue!

On our fourth day, I took Liz up to the top of the Empire State Building, which is a must for any tourist. Whilst taking in the fantastic views, I noticed a bank of telephones. I thought, "Who can I phone from the top of the Empire State building?" I decided to call Agent X, to say all was well… Thank heavens I did! In a voice of sheer panic, they said that they had been trying to reach me, as the BBC wanted me back to shoot that *Maybury* scene on Westminster Bridge in two days' time! Oh my God, now I'm panicking. We went straight to Freddie Laker's to see if we could get a ticket back to London. Thank heavens there was one for the next day otherwise I'd have had to pay for a full price one. There was no problem for Liz as we already had the tickets for LA, though I obviously had to forfeit mine. I went back to Cockroach House, got packed and called Barry, who promised to look after Liz and help her get to the airport.

Two days later, I'm back at BBC Television Centre, getting into my copper's costume. I don't say a word about my adventure! We go back to the same car park, I get back on the same coach, eat another bacon sandwich and once again wait for ages until the hours pass by and it's lunchtime. Eventually I get the script I had asked for last time. At last, I will finally know what I'll be doing. With minimal excitement, I start reading and looking for my dialogue. Page after page, nothing... not a word, nor a mention of PC Adam... Surely I haven't flown halfway around the world just to be the French Flag for the camera again?

Yes I had. After seven hours sitting on the coach, at 5pm I was called back to the same steps, once again with my back to camera, with the cameraman still moving me about to cast the shadow over the lens. "ACTION!" yells Don. The boat comes in... and exactly the same thing happens. The skipper shouts, "It's too shallow" and turns the boat around... Now I want to scream, but I can't say anything, because I can't reveal that I'd broken my contract by leaving the country. Don Taylor insists that the skipper does it again and this time brings the boat up to the steps, whatever the damage. "ACTION!!!" I have to admit that with the light fading by the second, I didn't hold out much hope for any success. I was proved correct, as the skipper refused to damage his boat. I was amazed that no one on the production team had done their homework on the Thames tides. If we had shot an hour earlier it would probably have been high enough.

Exactly the same reaction from Don Taylor, "I'm scrapping this scene!" I hoped I might get an apology, especially as my character didn't seem to be "integral" to the piece after all, but not a word was said. I went back to the BBC, got in the car and drove back to my empty house, while Liz was now with Liz Jamplis in LA. I phoned my agent and explained what had happened. "Please get me out of this." I happened to see Ray, our neighbour, who asked me what I was doing back so early. I told him the story and that I would be going to Heathrow tomorrow morning to find a flight to LA. Ray said, "Get a ticket now with British Airways and I will get you upgraded to First Class." I did a double take. "What?? How???" Ray revealed that he worked for the catering firm on the flights and that he could get me upgraded. The following day, I'm looking my smartest at Heathrow, boarding the plane and sure enough, Ray had got me upgraded and there I was in First Class. What a lucky man. Fantastic!

I felt so refreshed when I arrived at LA, where I was met by the two Lizzes and Jack X Field, Liz Jamplis' agent. We were staying in Liz J's apartment, while she was staying with her boyfriend. Her apartment had a garage underneath and I hired a car via her boyfriend, but when I tried to park it, I managed to hit the frame of said garage, causing quite some damage to it. Thankfully a neighbour, who obviously felt sorry for a Limey with no talent for driving, offered to repair it and did so for nothing. There are some really great Americans!

Jack X Field was an amazing man who spoke Chinese fluently and had even accompanied President Nixon on a trip to China. He was also a Communist during the period of McCarthyism and later decided to become a theatrical agent to a number of writers and performers who had been blacklisted for their beliefs and alleged involvement with the Communist party. So many famous people had their careers ruined and no one else would represent them until Jack took them on and helped them become successful in Hollywood once again.

Jack took to Liz and me and would drive us around in his blue convertible Cadillac, taking us to the best restaurants. One day, Jack and I were doubles partners at tennis, playing against two big Hollywood producers at an amazing property, where Charlton Heston had just finished a game before us! Jack lived in the Hollywood Hills and before I joined them in LA, the two Lizzes went to his house, where he revealed that he never locked his doors; his home was always open to friends. Apparently, he had never been burgled! Liz saw his telephone directory, which had the numbers for every movie star you could imagine, but to her credit she overcame the temptation to write any down.

What a fantastic time we had thanks to Jack and Liz Jamplis, who even got us into Disney World for free, before driving us down to Palo Alto, where we stayed with her parents. Her father was a cancer surgeon with his own clinic, and he took us all out for a lovely meal at Fisherman's Wharf in San Francisco! During those three weeks we were in California, our feet never touched the ground and we had an amazing time, which I felt more than made up for being a French Flag. But things got even better...

When we got home I received an apology from the BBC for my experience on location. I even got my full fee, despite not appearing. Then lo and behold, Don Taylor immediately cast me in his next production, a huge BBC *Play of the Month* adaption of Sheridan's *The Critic*, which featured an all-star cast (apart from me). My name even came up on the credits before Sir John Gielgud's! So all in all, I was glad that I had donned the uniform to play my first TV copper. Little did I know, that I would soon be doing this on a regular basis...

CHAPTER 16

Empty Your Pockets, Son

After my unforgettable turn as a PC Adam in *Maybury*, I had to wait a little while before I pounded the beat again. In the summer of 1981, I was back in the West End, performing at the Whitehall Theatre, as it was then known, in a production of the John Wells play *Anyone for Denis*. Set at Chequers during the time of Maggie Thatcher, the play centred around her husband Denis, played by John himself. The play was very successful and during its second year, John, who I had first met when he wrote a play for Joan Littlewood called *The Projector*, asked me to take over the part of Boris, the Russian spy who lived in a cupboard! I had one week's rehearsal, but without meeting any other members of the cast, including Angela Thorne who was playing Maggie T, as she was also filming the TV series *To The Manor Born* with Penelope Keith at the time.

I also didn't meet the director, Dick Clement, and so after rehearsing with the stage manager and Angela Thorne's understudy during the daytime, my only other chance to see what was expected of me was to watch the show every night for a week from the back of the circle. The character of Boris opened the play, seen planting a microphone in the tulips on a table, singing a Russian folk song as the curtain went up. I would also be playing the American Ambassador in the last scene. On my first night, I'll never forget Angela Thorne walking on stage. We hadn't rehearsed, nor even met to say hello, but here I was sharing the stage with her as she gave such a fantastic performance as the Prime Minister. When I think back, I am amazed that the producers allowed an actor to go on stage with so little help.

It was also during this production that Liz and I got our first dog, a Bull Terrier that we named Gimli, after the dwarf warrior in *Lord of the Rings*. We named most of our pets from that book! As Liz was working away from home sometimes, I had to take Gimli, who was still a puppy, with me to the theatre. He was still too young to meet other dogs, so I had to carry him from my parked car up to my dressing room, which I shared with Philip Martin Brown. Philip was great and didn't mind having Gimli with us. During every interval I would take Gimli up on to the roof of the Whitehall to let him have a wee!

In May 1982, Britain went to war in the Falklands and John decided that, quite rightly, he didn't want to make fun of the Prime Minister when our soldiers were dying thousands of miles from home, so the play closed. I then went into *Angels*, written by Tony Holland, who later co-created *EastEnders* with Julia Smith. Tony and I had shared a dressing at Wyndham's Theatre when we were in *Oh, What a Lovely War*. I was delighted that he thought of me for this nice part in a couple of episodes.

But after that busy period, I barely worked the following year at all, which continued into 1984. Eventually, I had a phone call from my agent asking, "What are you doing tomorrow?" I gave my usual response, "You should know... nothing!" I had an audition for a project I was very excited about; a new musical about the life of Laurel & Hardy called *Blockheads*. I have always been a huge fan of this iconic double act and I still have their autographs signed to me, which I collected at the Chiswick Empire when they were doing their last tour in 1957!

Blockheads had been dreamed up by the all-American team of writer Michael Landwehr, lyricist Hal Hackady and director Arthur Whitelaw. I remember being really nervous when I went to my audition at the Mermaid Theatre, as I wanted this so much. I was called to the stage and interviewed by Mr Whitelaw, who seemed nice and put no pressure on me to perform. Unbeknownst to me, he had directed a production of *Snoopy* for my cricketing friend Max Howard, who had recommended me. After a little chat, Arthur asked if I would sing something for him, so I offered him 'Soon It's Gonna Rain' from the musical *The Fantasticks*, a number I like because it's an easy song for a non-singer! I finished and I soon got the news that I had been cast in the musical! I would play three parts: Stan's father and film producers Hal Roach and Louis B Mayer. I was in heaven! Sadly, this feeling would not last long...

At the first day's rehearsal at the Mermaid, I met the rest of the cast, including Kenneth H Waller, an American actor bought over for the production especially to play Oliver Hardy, and a young English actor called Mark Hadfield who was to play Stan Laurel. Mark had been in the production of *Snoopy* that Arthur had directed, and I think it was he who tipped me off that our director had something of a reputation, earning him the nickname Mr. 'White-Lie'... I soon understood why. We read the script for the first time and it was honestly very badly written, the scenes had no flow to them, just a set of jumbled up sentences broken up by songs, which were definitely the best part of the musical.

As we left for home, I confided to Mark Hadfield that I felt we could make our scenes work with some adjustments to the writing. Mark agreed and I said I would have a go at making some suggested changes overnight, which we would then show to our esteemed director. I worked on the dialogue and presented my changes to Arthur, who thought they were good. I was now getting much more confidence in him, perhaps this would work out after all?

On the third day of rehearsals, we ran the first act with the writer watching. We then broke for lunch and on returning Mr Landwehr told us that we were reverting back to the original version and, in somewhat of a controlled rage, he told me not to change another word of his script... That was the beginning of the disaster that enfolded on what should have been a good fun show. Mr. 'White-Lie' did nothing to try and turn the production around, and in fact only gave me one note during rehearsals. "It's not funny. Make it funny".

When we opened, we had the customary first night party at the Criterion in Piccadilly. Present were many American investors who had put their money into this show and were understandably not looking too happy. When the negative reviews started to appear, both our director and author fled the scene, leaving behind Kay Cole, our excellent choreographer, to pick up the pieces. We never saw Landwehr and White-Lie again during the rest of the run and *Blockheads* closed after the obligatory two weeks. What a disaster!

Perhaps it was fate that I was back in the land of unemployed actors in the summer of 1984. Out of the blue, my agent received a call from Thames Television, asking if I would come and do a scene for a new police series, called *The Bill*. They would bike the script to me and get me details of what time and where I would need to go the next day. Straight offers are always nice for an actor, even at late notice. I of course agreed and lo and behold, a couple of hours later this script duly arrived. Written by Geoff McQueen, the episode was called *Funny Ol' Business – Cops and Robbers* and I was being asked to come in and do a half-page of dialogue in the very first scene, playing a duty sergeant originally called Edwards, who was finishing his shift. He was handing over to the next sergeant, called Cryer, updating him as to what had happened overnight, which prisoners were in each cell etc.

The next morning, off I went to Wapping, close to Tower Bridge. I drove there; in those days parking was simple, even up in town. I think I was called for 7.30am, as I had to have a police uniform fitted and the usual powder down and check that my hair was not too long to play a police officer! A lovely bonus for me was that the wardrobe department was run by two of Liz's friends, Jenny Tate and Mandy Harper. It's always a great comfort for an actor arriving in a new environment when you see someone you recognise. I got fitted very quickly and then went to meet Peter Cregeen, the producer of the series, who was also directing this episode. We had worked together a few times before and Peter was his usual charming self, thanking me for coming at short notice. He then introduced me to the actor I would be doing the scene with…

Blimey, it was Eric Richard! We had only recently finished doing a play together at the Theatre Royal, Stratford East called *Better Times*. *The Bill* was made using the rehearse-record technique, where after a quick run-through for the technicians, you would do your scene and then they would move onto the next. This approach petrified actors who were used to spending a week in rehearsal, which used to be standard practice in television. But I enjoyed this way of working, and after an hour, I had finished my scene on *The Bill*. Once again

OH, WHAT A LOVELY MEMOIR

Peter thanked me and I said my goodbyes to Eric, Jenny and Mandy, got in the car and I was back home before lunch! Driving home, I marvelled at how easy a gig it had been and wondered why I had been called in at the last moment.

A few weeks later, I got another call to say that Peter Cregeen would like me to come back, this time to do an episode called *Death of a Cracksman*, directed by Chris Hodson. I was playing the same character, though he would now be called Sgt. Alec Peters, as the surname Edwards had been given to Colin Blumenau's character Taffy. This time, I took the opportunity to ask Eric if he knew why I had come in last time at such short notice. He was a little reticent about telling me too much, as apparently the actor who had originally been cast in that part couldn't remember his lines. Out of respect, Eric quite rightly didn't name the actor in question. Years later, I did find out who it was, but similarly I have never named him, as it must have been an awful experience for him that day.

The Bill was a spin-off of a pilot called *Woodentop*, which had been made the year before as part of Thames' brilliant *Storyboard* series. From that pilot, Mark Wingett, Trudie Goodwin, Colin Blumenau and Gary Olsen returned to play the same characters for this initial 11-part series. It was supposed to have been 12 episodes, and in fact I filmed my part for a third episode, *The Chief Super's Party*, but production was halted by a technicians' strike and so it was shelved for a year. This did inadvertently leave the door open for my return, should the series prove popular enough to warrant a second series, which of course it did.

Not everyone who had worked on the *Woodentop* pilot had returned for this first series of *The Bill*. Eric Richard was a new addition to the cast, having replaced a similar character originally played by Peter Dean, who instead of finding fame in Sun Hill, found it on Albert Square in *EastEnders*. Similarly, Robert Pugh had initially played D.I. Roy Galloway, though he declined to return for the series and the part was then recast and John Salthouse made it his own. Changes of cast between pilot and series are common enough, as I had found out for myself when I'd made the pilot for *Coronation Street* (more on that later!) Rounding out the cast on this first series of *The Bill* were Nula Conwell, Peter Ellis, Ashley Gunstock, Robert Hudson, Jon Iles, Roger Leach, Tony Scannell and Jeff Stewart, who like me had all been brought in for the odd episode, before our parts began to grow as fantastic writers like Barry Appleton and Christopher Russell started giving us more to do. Lucky us!

These first hour-long episodes of *The Bill* were full of fantastic writing and proved to be very popular, so it was no surprise when we came back for a second series. All the established cast returned, except for Gary Olsen, who had been signed up to star in his own series for Channel 4 called *Prospects*. As I was still not on a regular contract at *The Bill*, I was able to do other series as well, one of which was *Prospects* where I was reunited with Gary for a couple of days filming on a Thames pleasure steamer! Whilst Alec and Dave Lytton might not have had a very happy relationship in *The Bill*, it was good to see Gary again and I was pleased that he had got his own series.

Anyway, back to life at Sun Hill, or to be more accurate Artichoke Hill, our main location in Wapping situated right next to where Rupert Murdoch's newspaper was printed. An old warehouse had been converted into our police station, complete with a garage for the police cars to be driven into. Occasionally, we were able to park our own cars there too! Also, as we were filming on location, Thames had to supply food, so the canteen seen in the programme was a fully practical one and that is where the cast and crew ate their lunch too. This was actually very convenient, as you can imagine how difficult it would have been for a team of fifty people looking for a café every day at 1pm! There was a pub on the corner of Pennington Street, just up from where we worked and more often than not, a few dedicated actors would go for a little tipple. But a problem arose when the staff at the News of the World went on a huge strike against Murdoch, naturally over wages. It became so noisy in the street that it was now impossible to control the sound and when a third series was commissioned, the production team were forced to find a new home for Sun Hill police station.

In 1987, the decision was made to move to Barlby Road, near Ladbroke Grove, and a very good one it was too. Our new building, which had previously been home to the famous Rootes car factory, was much easier for me to get to, with plenty of parking. These larger premises gave us all much more space to play with and even came with a snooker room, which we would use both on and off camera. It was at this point I was offered a contract and signed up to appear in every episode of the third series. Peter Cregeen sat me down and we talked about the character, fleshing out who Alec was and where he was going. It was great that he wanted my input. We decided that he was an old-school copper who wasn't enjoying the job anymore, as all the procedures had changed now that P.A.C.E. had come in, which meant a lot more paperwork and that he couldn't clip a kid around the ear for stealing an apple. So Alec was waiting for his retirement. I have often been asked how similar I am to Alec. I suppose I am a lot like him; I can be a bit lazy sometimes and I try to avoid doing too much work.

But I think you have to relate to the part you play, unless you are asked to play a violent or deeply unpleasant person, and a strength of *The Bill* was how much of ourselves we all brought to our characters, which the writers picked up on.

One of my favourite episodes to make in 1987 was *Brownie Points*, which had a very good script written by Christopher Russell, who in my opinion was the very best writer we had on *The Bill* at this time; he always added humour for the actors and was not afraid of a big cast of characters. Christopher wrote me this great scene where a group of Brownies were visiting the station and Alec takes their fingerprints... Mary McMurray, the director, asked me to improvise a bit of business with the girls. On the first take, I asked this young girl what her name was, and she said "Pandora". Not a name I was expecting, so I innocently replied that I would love to see her box... "CUT!" came the cry from Mary, who with a smile explained the sexual connotation of what I had said, which had honestly not occurred to me! Also, playing a prostitute in this episode was my great mate Toni Palmer, who was married to a name you will now be familiar with; the playwright and theatre director Ken Hill.

By the end of 1987, *The Bill* had become a major hit, regularly attracting over 15 million viewers. It was no small wonder that Thames wanted more and so a decision was made that in 1988, we would move into an earlier timeslot and go out twice a week, all year round. I must confess that I had never wanted to join what was effectively a "soap", in terms of the new format, though I didn't feel I could leave at that point. Someone who felt differently was John Salthouse, who decided not to continue. Stepping in as the new D.I. was Chris Ellison, who had made a few guest appearances before as Burnside.

In order to make a continuous production work, there would now be two units, sometimes three, making episodes in tandem. The cast was also expanded and we welcomed the likes of Barbara Thorn, Ben Roberts, Nick Reding, Eamonn Walker and Kevin Lloyd to the family. We all marvelled at the skill of our production scheduler, the brilliant Nigel Wilson, who really kept the whole machine running. A clever way Nigel made sure that we weren't all stepping on each other's toes was to commission stories set entirely outside the station, featuring two or three of the regular cast. An early example of this was *The Coop*, written by one of my favourite *The Bill* writers, Garry Lyons. This episode was very claustrophobic and saw Trudie Goodwin, Colin Blumenau and myself playing scenes in an appalling shed, where we were being held hostage at gunpoint, surrounded by chickens that were being treated very cruelly by the gunman. Most of these chickens were thankfully made out of rubber, but the real ones were very smelly. It was also bloody hot in that shed, so between takes Colin and I would stand outside to cool down and get away from the dreadful smell. At one point, we looked over and saw a guy fly tipping in the yard behind us. He then looked up and, seeing us in our police uniforms, did a runner! I got mistaken again as a real police officer whilst filming some driving scenes for this episode. I was sitting in the panda car, when a woman ran up and started banging on the window, telling me someone had collapsed at the station and I needed to come and help! We've all got stories like those.

I also loved being given the chance to play some comedy and usually in *The Bill* if anything was going to go wrong, it would often be because Alec had done something silly and made a right old mess, like when he arrested a whole platoon of navy personnel in the episode *Good Will Visit*. Another of my favourite writers on the series was Julian Jones, who gave me a very funny two-part storyline, which was quite rare for the show at the time. The first part, *It's Not Majorca*, saw Alec having a really chaotic day in custody and, after a ridiculous series of events, he ends up accidentally injuring a lay visitor, played by Zohra Sehgal. Then in the following episode, *Mending Fences*, Peters is assigned to look after the same lay visitor, now temporarily confined to a wheelchair, at a school fete. Alec manages to win her over, even helping by doing a spot of gardening for her, and for once he came away smelling of roses.

The green-fingered theme was also present in *Pathways*, which was perhaps my favourite episode. I am the biggest critic of my work, but after watching this story recently for the first time in 35 years, I was delighted with it. The plot revolved around Sgt Peters and WPC Brind, played by Kelly Lawrence, investigating a series of strange incidents surrounding a nearby allotment... Brian Bilgorri did a fantastic job finding our locations, all perfectly captured by our BAFTA-winning cameraman, the great Roy Easton. And how lucky I was that *Pathways* had been penned by the great scriptwriter Peter J Hammond, who had only recently joined *The Bill*. Peter's script really helped develop the compassionate side of Alec and showed how he worked when he took an interest. I really enjoyed working with Kelly Lawrence, who was a lovely actress and so easy to act with. I thought our scenes with Alan Perrin, who gave a brilliantly underplayed performance as a man hiding in his shed after his wife had left him, were some of the best I was ever given on *The Bill*.

Directing *Pathways* was Michael Ferguson, one of our longest-serving and best directors. Michael also became one of the producers when we moved into the half-hour episodes, alongside Richard Bramall. My favourite memory of Michael and Richard is when Jon Iles and I had a fun idea to do our own version of *It'll Be All Right On The Night*, with Jon doing his brilliant impression of Denis Norden, presenting a selection of out-takes from *The Bill*. We were permitted to make this video, which would be shown at our Christmas party, as long as we promised that the video would go no further – a directive I agreed with, as showing these out-takes on TV could have deflected from the strength of reality that *The Bill* had. It's a promise I have kept to this day, some 35 years later!

I got the go ahead to direct the video and the PAs gave me some reels of out-takes. I was also given a cameraman to shoot Jon's pieces to camera. I asked Michael Ferguson and Richard Bramall if they would be willing to make a cameo and fake a crash in the car park... unbelievably, they agreed! I got two derelict cars, which were normally used as dressing for street scenes where a staged incident was shot, from the props boys. We cleared a space in the car park, where Michael and Richard would both be going for the same parking space. It had to be done in one take... and they did it! They then both stormed out of their cars and acted as angry motorists! How many actors have had their producers do that for them? They were both wonderful and I think they were secretly thrilled to be asked. Richard and Michael, along with Peter Cregeen and the rest of the production team, were a major part of not only the success of *The Bill* itself, but also the harmony around the base at Barlby Road.

CHAPTER 17

My Sporting Life

Football played a big part of my time on *The Bill*. The programme itself usually dealt with the more unpleasant side of the sport, with Sun Hill coppers going toe-to-toe with football hooligans in episodes like *Just Call Me Guvnor* and *A Good Result*. Away from the drama, one of my favourite parts of the job was working with the publicity department to arrange for members of the cast to play in a huge number of charity games. There were so many times we had to disappoint members of the cast, as we were always overbooked. The one game that everyone wanted to play was at Wembley Stadium for *Children In Need*, where members of *The Bill* and *Coronation Street* casts joined forces to play against *EastEnders*. Representing Sun Hill in 1991 were Graham Cole, Peter Ellis, Huw Higginson, Sam Miller, Ben Onwukwe, Andrew Paul, Colin Tarrant and myself. I don't mind telling you that waiting in the tunnel to walk onto that hallowed ground was possibly the most nervous I have ever been in my life. I was 50 at the time! *The Bill* took us to many league grounds and it was always great fun. I hope we all managed to help raise a few pennies for charity along the way.

I first discovered football at Gunnersbury Prep, where as a fearless seven-year-old, I found scoring goals easy. Then when I was eleven, my friend Barry Knight, who was a born organiser, formed a football team, which we called The Sutton

Court Juniors. Also on the squad was our friend Tony Wotton, who was a fine player. Barry and I thought we were pretty good too! One game, I had to play in goal, as our usual keeper couldn't play that day. A Brentford scout happened to watch this game, which I hadn't realised until he asked me to go to Griffin Park for a trial as their goalkeeper! Needless to say, I didn't go for that trial, as I wanted to be a centre forward, though as captain of the Sutton Court Juniors, Barry always gave that part to himself! Barry joined us to a league played at Gunnersbury Park, where we had many a game.

The three of us also enjoyed going to watch football. Brentford FC was just down the road and we spent our Saturdays watching them. Sometimes, when Brentford were away, we went to Fulham. I do remember playing truant from Gunnersbury Prep on a Tuesday afternoon, when Brentford were playing Aston Villa in a cup replay. I wanted to go to that match particularly as Villa had a great centre half, Danny Blanchflower, and we had the legendary centre forward Tommy Lawton. There was a huge crowd at this game, and as I was a little boy, I got shunted to the front. It was very exciting for me to watch my heroes play before my very eyes, especially when I should have been at school. I felt really grown up as it was my secret and I never told my parents about my afternoon off, or anyone else for that matter, until now!

In my twenties, I played local league football for a team called Manresa, which was a teacher training college in Roehampton where my former drama teacher, and fellow lover of jazz, Tony Ford was studying. Knowing my love of all games, Tony invited me and Richard O'Sullivan to join them once for a game… I found myself staying for five seasons! I was now doing fairly well as an actor, so I really shouldn't have got so involved, as if I had broken a limb or a nose when I was halfway through a contract, all hell would have broken loose. Though we did do pretty well, even winning the league a couple of times. Richard only played a few times before I assume his agent got him out of it, but I made a whole new bunch of friends, one of whom was Jim Howard, a great bloke who went on to be a teacher. I was delighted when Jim asked me to be best man at his wedding.

But my sporting life has not just been limited to the beautiful game. Amongst the other sports I tackled at Gunnersbury Prep was rugby. This was not a game I was fond of playing, but as one of the fastest runners in the school, I was made to play on the wing, the idea being, 'give the ball to Dann and he will run and get a try!' I was only ten years old, but we were playing against schools with much older boys on their teams and I lost count of the number of times I got crunched to the ground by the bigger boys when I tried to score. Not my idea of fun! We also had a rather large lad on our side called Smith, who had the nickname 'Jumbo'. He really was much larger than any other boy I knew and he scored many, many tries. We would give the ball to Jumbo and he would make his way to the line with at least four lads trying to bring him down. He would be crying his eyes out while we encouraged him with cries of "Go Jumbo, Go!" Schoolboys can be evil. I often think of Jumbo Smith and wonder how he got on in life. I'm afraid to say that I never knew his real name.

The following year, I got in the school's first eleven cricket team. The rest of the team were fourteen-year-olds, but I was still only eleven. I used to assume that I was picked because our sports master, Mr Bright, who was also our maths teacher, thought I was able. I wish I'd asked Mr Bright at the time why he'd picked me, so I wouldn't still be wondering over 70 years later! I was so proud of my position in the school and it was great going to other schools to play. I never had a bowl, and very rarely got a knock, mostly fielding on the boundary. We had a fast bowler called Moss, who I remember once clean-bowling a boy and at the same time breaking one of the stumps in half! He later played for Middlesex and I believe he got a few games for England.

A junior boy at school, who I only knew by his surname Robertson, was the son of the England and Middlesex cricketer Jack Robertson! I never really talked to him, as he was two years younger than me, but I was impressed by who his father was. Many years later, my cousin Barbara cajoled me into playing for a local charity of hers. Lo and behold, it was announced over the Tannoy that Jack Robertson was in the crowd watching! I went to find him, and who should be there but his son as well. Robertson Jr. and I reminisced about out time at Gunnersbury, though I didn't have the heart to say I still didn't know his first name... but still, I had the privilege of meeting one of my cricketing heroes!

A sport I wasn't cut out for was boxing. Every year at Gunnersbury Prep, the inter-school boxing contest was held in the gym. The school was divided into four teams; North, South, East and West, which you would represent in every sport. I was in North and to my horror I was selected to represent them in the Class One category, which would include boxing! I can't remember the identity of the boy I had to fight, but I do remember that as we stood in the middle of the ring trying to punch the hell out of each other, we both started crying. I have no idea who won, but I surely lost some brownie points there!

One of the rules of the school was for all boys to purchase their school uniform from Barkers of High Street Kensington, an upmarket store and an overpriced one at that. Also, we had to have a nametag sewn onto the inside collar as well as on all our sports wear. Mine of course just read 'Dann'. Only a few days had passed when I returned home in my new jacket, which was filthy dirty and in a fairly disgusting state. I was severely told off and sent up to my room. Moments later, Mum came up to release me and pointed out that I had put on the wrong jacket, as once she had scraped off the mud and detritus, this one's label showed the name of 'Dunn'. A reprieve, thank heavens for that!

I remember my first Sports Day at school, where my parents came along to watch a gymnastic display. I was kneeling on the bottom row with a pyramid of my first form classmates kneeling on my back. I think we made a pyramid of almost two high and we were very proud to have achieved this. I also think it was the first time I had heard a round of apathy from my parents. Throughout the day, Mum was chatting away to another parent, as she could do. She told the story of this filthy jacket, which her son had picked up with the name Dunn in by mistake. She was obviously going over the top about how disgusting it was and questioned how a parent could allow their son to arrive at school in such a state. Not much was said in return, until Mum realised, "Where are my manners, I haven't introduced myself, I am Mrs Dann. I didn't catch your name..." It was Mrs Dunn.

When I was 14, I joined a Christian youth charity called Crusaders, where young men would meet at a hall in Chiswick every Sunday for religious instruction. Formed in the early 1900s, the organisation was renamed Urban Saints on its centenary in 2006 and is still going strong today. Now just to clarify, I am not and never have been a religious person, but the Crusaders had a good athletics ideal and a friend suggested that I would enjoy it. And he was right! We entered various competitions; the one I remember most fondly was at Merton Park for the National Crusaders meet. We entered the 4x4 relay and won the final by yards. It was only years later when I looked at the old programme, I saw that we had beaten a team that included David Hemery, future CBE and Olympic champion at the 1968 Summer Olympics in Mexico, where he won the 400 metre hurdles! I obviously claim it was me who ran against him during our relay race, but it was Martin Higdon, who later became a pole vaulter and British record holder.

Unlike David Hemery and Martin Higdon, my career was destined for the stage, rather than stadiums, and once my acting career was in full flight, it was a while before sport found its way back into my life. In 1978, I was asked by my old Corona mate Max Howard to be in his production of *Joseph and his Amazing Technicolor Dreamcoat* to be performed at Poole and directed by another old mate, Maurice Lane. The cast was full of young men playing the brothers and various other parts. Whilst rehearsing at a church hall in Holborn, there was an alleyway where, when we weren't needed, us boys would play cricket, albeit by bowling a tennis ball and using a piece of wood as a bat. By the time we were performing at Poole, we arranged a game of cricket against the parents of all the children who were needed for the production, which was great fun.

When the production finished, a few of us decided to form a team to play regular cricket, made up entirely of members who were connected with the entertainment industry. We struggled to think of what to call ourselves at first, until someone came up with the name Chadwick, which sounded like the name of a quaint English village. In fact, we were named after a street in Victoria where actors signed on for their employment benefit! The club is still going 40 years later. We started playing in Battersea Park, but after our first year we needed a permanent ground and we found one in Wimbledon at Merton Road. It was at one game we were playing there that a certain Jim Howard turned up. I hadn't seen Jim for years, not long after I was his best man in fact. We chatted after the game and I asked him where he had been. Sadly his marriage broke up fairly soon after the wedding, but he was newly remarried. I asked him to join Chadwick, even though he wasn't strictly an entertainer, although he played the guitar and could sing 'Puff the Magic Dragon'. Jim was a very fine cricketer and he won many a game for us.

As much as I love my cricket, I do feel I must apologise here and now to Liz, who became a Sunday cricket widow for a while. I was often in trouble for saying that I would rush back after a game for a party or dinner, but so many times I was late. Liz has always been a good sport though, and she did join me for a very memorable cricket trip during my time on *The Bill*, when I was asked to go to Gibraltar with the Lord's Taverners, a prestigious charity organisation. We had a hell of a time. There was to be only one game over the four days, with the rest of the time taken up by charity events, and alcohol, arranged by the Navy and other organisations. There were plenty of celebrities supporting the charity, including June Brown, who I hadn't seen since our time touring *The Taming of the Shrew*.

The cricket game itself was played on an all-weather football pitch, where it seemed the whole of Gibraltar came to watch. The team featured a selection of ex-professionals, including John Price, a former fast bowler who had played for England in 15 Test matches! I don't remember much about the match, where everybody had a go at bowling and batting, but it was during the game that John Price asked me to become a Taverner! The evening after the match was a special event, evening dress and all the fineries. That meant we'd had to bring an extra case with us, just for carrying my DJ and Liz's eveningwear. The venue was a cave, which had recently been cut out of the rock. That might sound bizarre, but it was an amazing "room" and absolutely huge, with plenty of space for dining and dancing. Liz and I made good friends that night with Bill Frindall and his wife Debbie. Bill was famous for his work as a scorer on BBC Radio's Test Match coverage, where he earned the nickname 'The Bearded Wonder' for his uncanny knowledge of obscure cricket facts. I asked him if he would like to become the President of Chadwick and he accepted, which earned me big brownie points back at the club. Plenty of wine was consumed that night and to be honest, I don't remember walking back to the hotel at the end of the evening. Fellow Taverner Chris Tarrant certainly didn't remember either, as he was so out of it that his wife refused him entry to their room and he had to sleep on a bench in the foyer! We had quite a laugh at his expense the next day.

Becoming a Lord's Taverner was one of the more positive results of the 'fame game'. One of the things that *The Bill* gave me was much more recognition from the public. Most of the time it was pleasant, though there were times when it was downright rude. I once had a van driver stop in the road and yell, "What's the matter with you! Don't you remember me?" When I tried to explain that we hadn't met and suggested that he might have seen me on TV, he took exception to this and threatened to bash me up. Most of the time it was fine, though Liz didn't like it when we were in a restaurant and fans would come up and push her out of the way to get an autograph. But even she got curious now and again about the fame that *The Bill* had brought her husband, so sometimes when we were out and about, she would walk behind me and then watch people as they turned to look at me... a bizarre hobby!

My favourite encounter happened when we had a holiday in Mauritius. We were sitting on the beach and a young boy, who could only have been 15, said to me, "You are a policeman." He knew very little English and was terribly nervous about talking to a foreigner. When I explained that I wasn't a policeman, he replied, "TV policeman". I couldn't believe it, I hadn't for a moment thought he was referring to Alec... was *The Bill* showing in Mauritius? Eventually he managed to explain that he had seen the programme while visiting family in England. I couldn't get away from Sun Hill!

When I was asked to play my first sort of serious game of cricket as a Lord's Taverner, I couldn't believe the calibre of only recently retired professionals I was playing with. All these ex-international players were very good to me and could see that I played a bit. I was usually put in to bat at around number 5, so I always got a game and they let me bowl my little left arm rubbish. I have a hundred stories about my efforts, but I will spare the gloating... except for one event.

We were playing in Birmingham against a very good club side, no quarter given. I batted quite well, not making many runs myself, but I stayed at the crease whilst the great West Indian batsman, Alvin Kallicharran, scored a fantastic hundred. Whilst fielding, I took a pretty good running catch on the boundary, then bowled and had three wickets, including one easy missed stumping from the lovely Indian keeper, Farokh Engineer. It was a pleasure having a laugh with him at his expense. At the end of the game, as I was leaving the field a gentleman sitting in the members' stand called me over. As I got nearer, I couldn't believe it: it was Sir Garfield Sobers, who to me was the finest all-rounder ever! He said to me, "You're a very fine cricketer, young man". I thanked this legendary player and walked away with immense pride. Young man? I was 50! That is the only 'crit' I will remember, as it beats any I got for my acting over my career. I still glow as I think back.

The Bill also opened doors for me to play in charity golf matches. These Pro-Am events were daunting for me as an average player, watching on as the likes of Nick Faldo and Ian Woosnam hit the ball a mile and it went exactly where they wanted. At the Dunlop Masters, I was the so-called 'celebrity' partner to Mark Mouland, the former British boys' golf champion. Mark kindly gave me some tips, though they didn't make much difference. I often attended these events with Tony Scannell, with whom I had shared many a round (of golf!) during our theatre days. Once, at a marvellous hotel we were staying at in Aberdeen, I was stood around the swimming pool chatting to some of the great golfers we would be playing. Then Tony turned up in his evening dress and dived straight into the pool, dickie bow and all!

As I write this book aged 82 (playing age 43!) I am still pretty fit, partly thanks to joining Walton-on-Thames' Walking Football club, organised by Mark Blythe. I still score the occasional goal, though I get more pleasure these days as a defender stopping the opposition from scoring! The banter is brilliant, especially when we all have a coffee afterwards, and we have played several tournaments in Portugal. Great fun!

CHAPTER 18

Roger, Over and Out

As an actor, there are times when you join a company, either going for a read-through of a television script or to the first rehearsal of a play, where you know almost straight away that the chemistry between the company is good and therefore, this will benefit the production. I definitely had this reaction when I joined *The Bill*, we very quickly become a big happy family. I made great friends with Roger Leach, who played Sergeant Tom Penny. Roger was Australian, which people were often surprised by, because you could never hear a trace of that accent in his performance. That didn't surprise me of course, because right from the off I recognised that he was a great actor.

Roger lived in Salisbury, Wiltshire, with his wife Brenda and their son Ben. It used to be a very long journey for him to Barlby Road and when the decision was made to turn *The Bill* into an ongoing bi-weekly series, it would have been impractical for Roger to do that commute 52 weeks a year. To save him from either an exhausting commute or staying in expensive digs, Liz and I invited Roger to stay with us at our home in Hampton Hill. It would only take us about twenty minutes to drive to the studio first thing in the morning and then when we got home, we had a choice of five pubs within a short stagger from our front door. I would often find Roger down one of these locals after work, reading his Guardian.

OH, WHAT A LOVELY MEMOIR

It is often thought that actors who work on a series must be busy on set 100% of the time... Well, I am willing to break that rumour, as we are of course not in every single scene being shot and therefore have a lot of time to gaze at our navels. This gets you nowhere, and so Roger and I decided to see if we could write; not only episodes for *The Bill*, but invent our own ideas for different series... One of our ideas was *The Motor Traders*, a six-part comedy series about a daughter who inherits her late father's car garage. She attempts to make the business her own, but is plagued by his advice from beyond the grave, regularly hearing his ghostly voice emanating from the urn containing his ashes on the mantelpiece. Roger used to do the typing on his Amstrad, because he was fifteen times faster than me, while I walked up and down the room, coming up with dialogue. I really enjoyed that period of my life spending time with Roger.

When it came to writing scripts for *The Bill*, we had been told as a company that the actors should have no say in the direction or writing of the series, under any circumstances. I know that Roger and I weren't alone in our ambitions to write for the series and I later learned that both Colin Blumenau and Jon Iles submitted storylines, which I am sure would have made very fine episodes. Nowadays, there is nothing unusual about seeing actors getting involved behind the scenes and writing, directing or even producing the series they are starring in. But back when we were on *The Bill*, despite it being a ground-breaking programme in so many ways, this was certainly not an option.

Roger and I were determined to try and get an episode on-screen and so the writing duo of Stephen Stratford and Anthony Forbes were born, our pseudonyms made up partly from our middle names. We were also careful not to include anything in our stories for either Tom Penny or Alec Peters, as that really would have given the game away. We wrote scripts for two episodes, plus a story outline for a third. First came *A Testing Time*, which would have seen Carver and Lines recruiting Ackland to go undercover to investigate a driving test scam. Our second script, *Ladies Of Distinction*, would have seen Inspector Frazer successfully taking charge of a siege, while Brownlow, Conway and Burnside were all away enjoying a boozy lunch over at Scotland Yard.

We spoke to Barbara Cox, one of the script editors on *The Bill*, in confidence and explained that we had written these episodes and asked if she would like to read them. She did, and to our great delight she loved them! Barbara said that she would like to officially commission us, but that it was imperative that Michael Chapman, who had now taken over from Peter Cregeen as Executive Producer, must not find out that we had written these episodes! Barbara felt that having two pseudonyms made up of our middle names was a little too obvious, and so Victoria Hampton was born. Her name was a combination of Victoria Avenue, where Roger lived, and Hampton Hill, where I lived. We were duly paid for the first two scripts and the Canadian Bill Brayne was assigned to direct the episodes.

A director on *The Bill* was employed for a six-week contract; one week to prepare an episode, one week to shoot it, then a week to edit it. This would then be repeated for the second episode. It was during the pre-production of our first episode, *A Testing Time*, that Bill Brayne went into the office and asked Barbara if he could meet with Victoria, to have a chat about a couple of things that he wanted clarified. It was then he was told who Victoria was and the strict rule of no interference from the actors was explained to him, which he completely understood. To this day I don't know how, but Mr Chapman found out and despite having read the script and giving it the go ahead, he pulled our episodes from production and they were never made. Amazingly, we still got our fee for writing the two scripts, plus our outline for a third, but as far as Mr Chapman was concerned, Roger and I became personae non gratae.

I never asked Roger if this was the reason why he decided to leave *The Bill* the following year in 1990. By this time, the production had moved to Merton, as sadly the lease ran out at Barlby Road. This was a real shame as there had been an excellent atmosphere there and it was genuinely always a pleasure to go to work there. To help with the move, an episode called *Trojan Horse* was written, in which a car bomb exploded and caused devastation to the station, resulting in the death of PC Melvin, played by my good friend Mark Powley, who I was sorry to see leave. The following episodes then saw Sun Hill station being rebuilt, which helped disguise the fact that we had moved to Merton; a very clever move spearheaded by Nigel Wilson and the design team. I'm not sure how many of the audience would have realised this at the time.

With respect to the programme, and to all my friends and colleagues involved, after playing Alec for five years it had now become rather repetitive. I like to be challenged as an actor, but sadly after the move to Merton, it felt like Alec spent most of his time in the station as custody sergeant, saying the immortal words "Come on son, empty your pockets". I didn't feel like the part was going anywhere, and to be honest I had fallen out of love with the job and had started doing it primarily for the money. We weren't paid the salaries that actors on the likes of *Casualty* are paid today, but it was a regular wage and meant that we could build an extension on the house and do things like that. But like Roger, I felt it was time to leave.

ROGER, OVER AND OUT

Fate took a hand in this, as not long into my stint at Merton, I was asked to go to Canada and direct a farce called *A Cuckoo in the Nest*, which was to be the first production of the 1991 season at the famous Shaw Festival Theatre in Niagara-on-the-Lake. It was not only a great honour for me to be asked, it was exactly what I needed to get my creative juices flowing again. I talked to my agent and explained that I wanted to do this. With his agreement, I handed in my notice at *The Bill*, telling them that I had this great opportunity and couldn't turn it down. I made no mention of how angry I still felt about what had happened to Roger and me with our scripts.

I had about three months left on my contract, which I was willing to fulfil, but I explained I would need a week off during this time to go to Canada to meet my designer and technical staff, before I started work on the play. I was then called into the casting office at *The Bill*, where they (not Michael Chapman) explained that they didn't want me to leave the programme. They offered to continue to pay my weekly wages for the two months I would be away in Canada, on the basis that when I returned I would begin a new contract with a rise in pay. I genuinely pondered on this, as I had enjoyed every second of working on *The Bill* at Artichoke Hill and Barlby Road. I spoke to Liz about what I should do and, as usual, she said she would support me whatever I decided. I made the decision to take the devil's shilling and stay.

The best thing about this decision was an excellent episode written by Russell Lewis called *Cry Havoc*, in which Alec was stabbed whilst trying to apprehend a suspect and almost died. This allowed me to be written out of the production for eight weeks, whilst Alec was away recovering from this trauma. In the end, they rearranged the running order and I was only off-screen for a month. I am proud to say that this episode is the top rated on IMDb, out of all 2,400 episodes of *The Bill*. Congratulations to director Stuart Urban, Roy Easton the cameraman, and all the crew. The cast weren't bad either, with a young Marc Warren playing the villain who stabbed Alec, pursued by Jonathan Dow as PC Barry Stringer, who impressively performed his own stunts in a daring sequence shot by Roy, hundreds of feet up on the gantry of the then derelict Battersea Power Station.

On my return from Canada, a fabulous episode was written for me by Tim Vaughan, our former script editor who was now writing for the programme under the pseudonym Victoria Taylor (maybe Victoria Hampton inspired him?). The episode was called *Addict* and saw Alec being dropped off back to work by his wife Angela (who had been introduced in *Cry Havoc*) played by Prim Cotton. Chris Lovett, who directed many episodes for *The Bill*, said he thought this episode was his best yet and he was really pleased with my performance. I was now feeling really glad to be back! But that didn't last long...

A week later, the producer, Peter Wolfes, called me up to his office. He had just watched the final cut of *Addict*, and said, "What do you think you are doing? That is the laziest performance I have ever seen." I was mortified; I couldn't believe what I had just heard. I don't believe I have ever given a lazy performance. He gave me the tape and told me to go and watch it. I went to the viewing room and put the video in with some trepidation. I don't like to blow my own trumpet, but I thought it was pretty good. I went back into Peter's office, tape in hand and calmly said, "I totally disagree with you. Alec has just returned from a near-death experience and basically he's scared of ever going out there again. He's still in pain and wants to be anywhere but Sun Hill. Considering how the writer had approached the story, I thought my performance worked." Peter snapped at me, "NO! Our audience is not interested what happened a month ago, get a grip!" I left the room feeling like Alec, wishing I were anywhere else but Merton Studios. Fortunately, when the episode was shown, it was well received, but I now totally regretted my decision to stay.

During the following year, I got very little to do, with Alec barely stepping foot outside the station. Then in the autumn of 1991, I got a letter from Michael Chapman, giving me three months' notice that my contract would not be renewed. I thought he might have told me to my face, but I found out other actors were given the same treatment. I have to admit that I did then get a couple of very fine episodes, including one by Julian Jones, who had previously written *It's Not Majorca* and *Mending Fences* for me. This new episode was called *Chicken*, which was about kids playing on a train line. Peters is on his way to stop them, but doesn't get there in time and he sees one of them run down and killed.

Alec then transfers 'upstairs' to a new post, but I was still under contract for another two months and was barely used. Eric Richard described it best, that "I went upstairs for a pencil and never came down." I was never properly written out and those last two months were purgatory for me, especially as Michael Chapman completely ignored me. The feeling was mutual, I had never been so unhappy in all my time on the programme. I was told that one of our producers went into Michael's office and had a big shouting row with him and was heard saying, "Why are you letting Larry go, he's one of our best characters!" I was flattered to hear this, but by this point I couldn't wait to leave.

OH, WHAT A LOVELY MEMOIR

I remember my last day filming was on a Saturday. When I finished my last scene and heard "Cut!", I went back to my dressing room that I shared with Eric, which we had previously shared with Roger. I took two stick-on nameplates from the door: mine, and another that read "Gimli (PC Sniffer)", as I used to bring him to the studio with me. He once stopped filming when he came onto the set to find me! I changed out of my uniform for the final time, cleared away my personal possessions and walked past the empty production offices on the flight deck on my way out. There wasn't a soul around, just my luck to finish on a weekend. Nearly eight years and no one there to say goodbye... but unbeknownst to me, a farewell party had been arranged at our local pub one evening during the following week. There were lots of nice speeches and presents, including the largest golf bag you could imagine, which I could never carry with all my clubs in, because it was so heavy. I wonder how those caddies manage! Best of all, Roger Leach had travelled up from Salisbury to be there at my leaving party. What a fantastic farewell all my mates gave me that night. Those wonderful people had became a huge part of my life and that party took away so much of the misery I had felt during my last days on the programme. Thank you all, you know who you are!

But this wasn't to be my final outing as Alec... You can imagine my great surprise when over a decade later, I received a phone call out of the blue, asking me if I would return for one more episode. It would basically be a three-hander between myself, Eric and Simon Rouse, who I had never worked with on *The Bill*. The story saw the three of us attending the funeral for Ted Roach, who had been played by the amazing Tony Scannell. Ted had died off-screen in an accident, after supposedly relocating to a village in the country. Cryer found it strange that a character as raucous as Roach would have opted for a quiet life, so the three of us start poking around and sure enough, we discover that his death is suspicious.

The script was by the brilliant Peter J. Hammond, who had written the marvellous episode *Pathways* for me all those years previously. By this point in 2004, *The Bill* had very much become a soap and had done away with episode titles, so this was one simply titled *Episode 248* (doesn't have quite the same ring to it as the fantastic titles we had in my day does it?) But it was such fun to do, especially working with a lot of the same crew who were working on the programme in my day. We were filming in a little village in Sussex, miles away from the base at Merton. I didn't particularly want to go back to the studio, though of course I had to go in and meet the wardrobe department and work out what I was going to wear. I felt really strange walking back into that building, which had changed so much. The studio even had a reception area now, I suppose for security reasons. After my fitting, I left and didn't go looking around for old times' sake.

The week away filming was really enjoyable, and it was great working with Simon and sharing scenes with Eric once again. The only thing that could have made it better was if Roger had been with us. Imagine if we could have reunited the original three Sun Hill sergeants together to solve one last case. Sadly this wasn't possible, as dear Roger had passed away in 2001, after suffering with a nasty cancer that killed him very quickly. The last time I saw him was when I was doing a pantomime in Bath, only an hour from Salisbury and so we arranged to meet for a drink halfway. Poor Roger looked really ill and he died a week later, bless his heart. He was a great guy and a very clever man; I saw him give some fabulous performances on stage after he left *The Bill*. And would you believe, we did eventually get a script on television!

In 1992, Pat Sandys, who as producer in charge of the Blue Unit was known to us all as "Mother Blue", had recently left *The Bill* to produce *EastEnders*. Pat had read the unmade episodes that Roger and I had written and asked us if we would like to write an episode for the gang at Albert Square. "Why not?" we thought, and so we did… Wow, was it hard work! Neither of us had watched it for years, especially whilst we'd been so busy on *The Bill*. We were sent the scripts for the previous ten episodes to the one we were to write, given an outline of the storylines we had to continue and where we could put in a few scenes of our own…

We were told certain things we had to do, one of which was to not give a certain actor many lines, as he had trouble learning them. Unfortunately for us, his part was the largest in the ongoing storyline! Another requirement was there had to be three scenes with a young couple, who were having a bad time with their relationship. But there was a problem with the actors' schedules, which meant that one of them could only do location scenes whilst the other was limited to the studio, meaning the two of them couldn't actually be together to do their scenes! In the end, we set two scenes on the phone and one at a front door on the Square, with one of them in the studio looking out, and another on location looking in… so even if they didn't meet, at least the door got some good close-ups!

I can't remember how many rewrites we had to do, as we kept being sent changes to the plot or the characters. When the episode was broadcast, we watched it and were amazed that it worked. We thought it safer not to have our names on it though, and dusted off Anthony Forbes and Stephen Stratford for their television debut as screenwriters. That would also be their final outing, as we decided "Never again" when it came to *EastEnders*. Roger did however get a couple of his solo *The Bill* scripts made and we continued to try and get a few of our other ideas off the ground, though sadly none of them ever came to fruition. It became harder now that Roger was living back in Salisbury permanently and this was before the days of FaceTime!

Away from his acting and writing achievements, Roger suffered from terrible claustrophobia, which meant he couldn't drive through a tunnel or fly, so when he travelled from Australia, he came by boat! When he wanted to take his wife Brenda and their son Ben to Australia to show them where he'd grown up, he realised he would need to fly, so he went to see a hypnotherapist, who cured him, meaning he was able to take his wife and son to Australia by plane. He fought claustrophobia and he won, which was amazing. Everything about Roger was brilliant, he was a great guy and I still miss him.

When I left *The Bill* in 1992, I had been offered a leading part in a film to be shot in Russia. The story was about a train breaking down in a station in the middle of nowhere, with a very important Russian general on board who was sick and needed help. I was to play the stationmaster, while my good mate from *The Bill* Peter Ellis was to play the general. Needless to say, the money to make the film never appeared and we didn't get to go to Russia. Same old story?

I wasn't out of work for long, as my old mate Ken Hill asked me to return to Stratford East and take over from Geoffrey Freshwater in *The Invisible Man*, which was to transfer to the West End. Ken's play featured over 100 wonderful illusions, which I had already enjoyed as a punter. I hadn't a clue as to how these amazing tricks were done, but I soon learned! I had to sign a Magic Circle form saying that I would never tell, and I never have. In the first half I played PC Jaffers, the incompetent policeman who gets strangled by the Invisible Man at the end of act one. This was great fun to do, as I had to wrestle with myself as I was being strangled. In the second act, I played the evil Dr Kemp, who wanted to get the secret elixir that made Dr Griffin invisible. It was always great fun working with Ken; I think we did 25 productions together!

Sadly, during this period my father got ill and was never able to come and see the play. He was in hospital in Gosport near where he lived. The NHS staff were excellent and allowed him to come and live with Liz and me for his final days. He was bought to our house by ambulance and lived with us for two weeks. Dad had lung cancer, not helped by his many years of smoking a pipe, I am sure. We had to arrange for oxygen tanks to be delivered, which he used continually as he had such difficulty breathing. He even needed this to be able to sleep. Despite knowing he was going to die, he never once complained. My brothers John and Ian helped Liz look after Dad while I was at the theatre, which I felt guilty about. John was great, staying up through the night to look after Dad. One night, I arrived back from the theatre to find Liz waiting for me at the front door. Dad had died. I hadn't said farewell before I left that day, as I thought he had more time. The next morning, I phoned the company manager and she told me to take the day off and only come back when I felt able. That night was the first and only time that I ever needed an understudy.

CHAPTER 19

A Year To Forget

At the beginning of 1995, I was in rehearsal to play Ramon in Ken Hill's production of *Zorro The Musical!* This very exciting venture was written by Ken, who added lyrics to the music of the Masters of the Zarzuela. Sadly, it soon became clear that Ken was not well; in fact he was very sick. He had a cancer that was restricting his heart and making it incredibly hard for him to find any energy to even walk. The rehearsal period was therefore, as you can imagine, quite traumatic. To make matters even more difficult, his wife Toni Palmer was also in the production. I personally don't know how she coped. They were staying in a little hotel nearby and Toni would drive Ken to and from the theatre every day, which in itself was a challenge, as it was hard for Ken to get in and out of their little sports car. I will never forget the occasion when at the end of one day, Toni asked me and Andy Secombe to help her get Ken into the car. This was not easy, as poor Ken's struggle was awful and he was hardly able to breathe. Andy and I really worried how Toni would cope back at their hotel.

We all arrived the following morning to continue with Ken's wishes to get the show on, as there was great hope for a transfer to the West End. We were rehearsing in the then unused Stratford Court House, just down the road from the Theatre Royal. We were surprised to find that Ken was not there, which was a first as he was always there before anyone else doing his preparation work. There was no sign of Ken, or Toni. It must have been about 11am when Philip Headley, the artistic director of Stratford East, came into the room and told us that Ken had died. The shock was enormous; we knew that he was really struggling, but we honestly thought that he would make the opening night and see us through to the West End. Phil told us to all go for an early lunch and come back by 2pm, when he would inform us all what we would be doing. Andy and I went to the pub we used to frequent over the railway bridge and had a couple of brandies, hardly able to say anything to each other. The rest of the fairly large cast went their own ways. No one could be sure of the future of *Zorro*.

We returned at the allotted time and Phillip told us that the show would go on, as Ken had wished. Ken had received excellent support from Peter Rankin, his assistant director for over twenty years. Peter had sat by Ken's side throughout rehearsals, filtering information to the cast whenever Ken couldn't cope. Philip announced that Peter would take over as director and that we would still open on 4 February as planned, which we did. The show ran until 25 March when it closed, never to be performed again! Our American backers pulled out, I believe because of Ken's death, meaning this fantastic piece of theatre never got to fulfil what I believed would have been a good run in the West End.

Sadly, during this already tragic production, my own life became a horror show. I remember very little from this period, except that on 20 February, my brother John was due to take my mother to hospital for a check up, but he couldn't get an answer at her door. He didn't have a key, but he knew that I did, so he phoned and asked me to come over and help. I rushed there both fearing the worst and puzzled, as the night before I was at her flat with many others celebrating her 78th birthday. I opened the door into her apartment and there she was. At first I thought she was fast asleep, but no, she had died. I phoned the police to ask for advice and they sent over a couple of coppers, who then called a doctor. I phoned a cricketing mate, who happened to be an undertaker. By now it was getting close to me having to be at the theatre, where because we had no understudies, I had to go on. I'm not sure if I told anyone what had happened, I think I was on autopilot. That night, and every night in the show, I had a duet with Toni, and I swear I had a tear in my eye every time we sang together. How she coped I will never know. How was I to cope? All I could think every day was "get to the theatre on time".

Unbelievably, on 24 March, the day before the show was to close, I had to have Gimli, my best friend and most brilliant dog, put to sleep, as he had a brain tumour. Saturday came, two shows, matinee and evening, the final curtain came down and I collapsed on stage. I have no idea what I did during that awful time - just do the show and grieve. As the eldest brother, I suppose I felt it was my responsibility to arrange my mother's funeral. To this day I can't remember where we had the wake, or who was there. They say bad news comes in threes, but for me in 1995, it was four. My mother's funeral was also the last time I saw my brother John, who died in his sleep on 6 June.

John lived on a barge on the Grand Union Canal in Southall, a wonderful space that he filled with good furniture he'd collected, as well as all his books and guitars. He had just bought a farmhouse in France and was going with Sian to live there and turn a barn into a studio for his music. On the day that he died, Sian was taking her driving test and if she passed, they were going to go straight away to France and start their new life. Their Dormobile campervan was already packed and ready to go. John had sold his barge and was staying on a friend's boat. Sian passed her test, but when she got back to the boat, she couldn't wake him up. She phoned me and I raced to Southall, to find John lying on a bunk bed, his face as white as a sheet, looking like he had put up a fight not to die. As I had just a few months earlier for Mum, I called the police, a doctor and my mate the undertaker. We did have a fantastic funeral for John, a non-religious ceremony with many of his friends attending. They sang some of his songs, told stories and we had a few laughs. That's the way to go. I still miss John. After he died, I sold one of his guitars to Eric Clapton via a friend who knew him.

 I had now got to the point in this year from hell where I didn't want to go out. I stopped taking part in golfing games. In fact, I remember trying to play in a match for my society club, but literally walked off not halfway through. I couldn't cope, I didn't want to meet or talk to anyone and I found it difficult to walk anywhere. During this time, poor Liz, who was still coming to terms with the loss of our great friend Gimli, kept asking me if I was all right. I of course said yes, even though deep down I knew something was wrong. I was having a breakdown. I didn't tell Liz, but I decided to go to the doctor and ask for help. The surgery was only about two hundred yards down the road, but it took an effort for me to get there. I went in and asked to see my doctor, but he wasn't in. The receptionist realised that something was wrong with me and said that another doctor would see me. I'll always remember her name, Dr Pennycook. She sat me down and right away I broke down in tears, speaking for what felt like ages, telling all my woes that I hadn't let out to anyone else. She asked me if I would like to have an appointment with a psychiatrist. I gave it a thought, but suddenly realised I already felt so much better, having shared my distress with this total stranger. I politely declined and reassured her that I felt fine and thanked her for listening to me. I walked home as if nothing had happened for all those months. I learned a big lesson: if in doubt, talk to someone, don't bottle it up.

But this year from hell still had more challenges in store for me. Later in the year, I got a phone call from an actor who had been in *EastEnders* for many years and was also with my agent (who for the purposes of this book we shall refer to as Agent X). This actor asked if Agent X had sent me all my residuals from repeats of *The Bill*. I said that I thought so and enquired as to why he was asking. It turned out that this actor was missing over £30,000 in sales. He had received a huge tax bill from HMRC, but had not received a penny of the associated residuals from Agent X. I then remembered that I had not yet received my fee for an episode of *Sooty & Co*, which I had shot some ten weeks earlier. Agent X had simply said that Granada was bad at paying and that they were chasing them up. I took the actor's phone number and told him I would make some enquiries...

By this time, I had been out of *The Bill* for three years and had received the occasional repeat payment. I thought it best to check directly and so I phoned Thames' actor's payments department, explained who I was and asked if they could tell me how much money I should have received over the last three months. The very helpful lady said that she would send me the details by post, with all copies of the relevant forms.

The forms came very quickly and I couldn't believe what I read... there was money missing, not too much, but enough to worry me. I phoned the actor to tell him what was happening and immediately got back on the phone to the helpful lady at Thames and shared my concerns. I asked her if she could send me details of all residual payments made to my agent from the day I left *The Bill* in February 1992 to the present day. About a week later, I got this huge envelope from Thames TV, with pages and pages of invoices. Just like the actor from *EastEnders*, I discovered that I was missing just over £30,000! I was shaking with anger as I phoned the office to speak to the agent. The phone rang and was answered by Brenda, Agent X's loyal secretary, who revealed that she had been alone in the office for weeks. I told her what I had found out and she revealed that she hadn't been paid herself for many weeks. It was then that I contacted the offices of *Sooty & Co* directly to ask if they had sent my payment through to Agent X and, of course, they had.

The continual problem for most actors is that we only receive payment from employers *after* it has been sent to the agent, who will first take their percentage and then, we hope, send us the rest of the money. This whole process is based on trust and, as I learned, is sadly all too easy for fraudsters to exploit. You hear of this happening a lot, but you never believe it will happen to you. I booked an appointment to see a lawyer at Equity, the actors' union. He was not aware of the problem, but would look into it and try to get my money back. Later on, I got a call to say that they couldn't find Agent X and that other actors on their books had also suffered the same thing, but it was me, and the *EastEnders* actor, who had lost the most income. They said there was nothing more they could do and that we just had to hope that Agent X could be found or gave us our money back. I later left this completely useless union.

I followed up with Agent X's loyal secretary and advised her to shut up shop and let the lawyers sort it out. Poor Brenda, a real darling who had been taken for a ride by someone she had worked with for as long as I could remember. In fact, I had known them for over twenty years; they had been a guest at our wedding! But as luck would have it, not much time had passed before Liz was working on a *Poirot* and was chatting to one of her costume colleagues about what had happened to me. An extra overheard the conversation and approached her, "Liz, I met you, your husband and your dog Gimli when I came to your house with the agent you are talking about...' Unbelievable! Liz asked if she knew where Agent X was and she explained what a bastard they had been to her mother, leaving her with huge bills after fleeing to live with a new conquest. She gave Liz an address.

I informed Equity and they finally got hold of Agent X, who nonchalantly said that they couldn't pay all that was owed and if Equity took them to court, they would claim bankruptcy and not pay back a penny. Equity said that we should try to get as much as we could and not go down the legal route. Reluctantly, I accepted a payment of £17,000. This money apparently came from Agent X's new lover, rather than their own pocket! I have to say that if ever I saw this person again, I would love to put one on their chin. Heaven knows how much was stolen from me over the many years that I trusted them. Would you believe they even asked for their usual 15% fee from the £17,000... they didn't get it!

After this, I asked my great mate Kaplan Kaye if he would represent me. He was mainly involved with the music business, but had a few actors on his books. He got me plenty of work doing all the commercial gigs that actors do after leaving a successful TV series, including a lot of pantomimes. It was by no means the best work I have been involved in, but it all paid well for a time until my fame as Alec finally disappeared from public view. Even though I am now happily retired, if by chance Spielberg wanted me to star in his next film, I would definitely get Kap to do the deal!

I mentioned earlier that I did an episode of *Sooty & Co*. I have often been asked, "What is the most fun you've ever had on a set?" Well *Sooty & Co* is the answer to that question, which when you consider this year from hell that I would otherwise wish to forget, is quite a compliment to the little yellow bear and his friends. I remember watching *Sooty* with my brothers in the 1950s, with Harry Corbett getting the water pistol treatment, Sooty whispering in his ear and then thumping Harry's head with a rubber hammer! Good fun violence for the kids. Well when I was asked if I would like to do an episode, of course I said yes. A few weeks later a contract came, outlining a couple of days' work in Manchester at the Granada studios, with a nice hotel for the overnights and a reasonable fee.

I was invited to play Mr Dwain ("as in Dwain Pipe") a civil servant from the council who has lost his memory. The rest of the plot was irrelevant, but it obviously involved Sooty and Sweep, with the help of Soo, taking me to the cleaners - not financially, but the Sketchley variety! I ended up having my head plunged into several chocolate gateaux... Wonderful! I gave Mr Dwain a high pitched, back of the throat voice. He would laugh at anything and wore a pair of joke glasses.

By the time I worked with Sooty, Harry Corbett had sold the franchise to his son Matthew, who was now Sooty's right-hand man (literally!) Now the thing to understand if you haven't had the pleasure of seeing the show is that Sooty communicates by whispering, either to Matthew or to Sweep, a grey fluffy dog, who then translates what Sooty has said with a squeaker noise. This would then be translated further by Soo, a little panda who spoke in a beautiful upper crust English accent, performed for many years by lovely Brenda Longman.

Mr Dwain's appearance in this episode, *Treasure Hunt*, went down well and I was asked to return for the first episode of the next series, *New Water*, and then again in 1997 for *Magic Mayhem*, where I ended up getting covered in that wonderful stuff known as "gunge". By this point, Matthew had been doing Sooty for a very long time and it was after this third episode that he revealed that he was retiring from Sooty and had sold it to Richard Cadell, a talented young man who was connected to the funfair business. Matthew asked me if I would come back next year to help ease Richard in. I was flattered, as he obviously thought that Mr Dwain was a useful foil. And so I returned for the episode *Psychic Soo*, where this time Mr Dwain had two children, a little boy and a girl who had to talk in the same silly voice as me. Once again, Mr Dwain came off worst, with food spilt all over me. I thought Richard Cadell coped really well picking up the baton from Matthew, who was now making cameo appearances in the series.

Not long after, I was invited to Matthew's leaving party at Granada Studios, where they very kindly gave me a room at the hotel opposite. It was a fantastic night, with lots of food, music and entertainment. After Matthew retired, I thought that would be the end, but I was lucky to be invited back by Richard for his new show, *Sooty Heights*, where the gang were now running a hotel. This time I played an outrageous character called Winston Ogilvie Whalley, a man who hated dogs and was canvassing for votes in the local council elections. I finished my five-year association on the longest-running children's show in the world with a funny bit of business, with Winston announcing, "I shall be the people's Whalley!" before walking straight into a door! Thanks for the gigs Sooty, and for cheering me up when there hadn't been a lot of fun in my life.

The Dann Brothers in 1995 (L-R) me, Ian, John and Richard after spreading Mum's ashes. This was sadly the last time we were all together, as John died three months later.
(Author's Collection)

CHAPTER 20

An Actor Retires...

After I left *The Bill*, I had high hopes of getting my teeth stuck into some new plays. The closest to this I got was starring in a number of plays for BBC Radio 4, including a *Thirty Minute Theatre* called *Virtual Radio* by Andrew Dallmeyer and a *Saturday Playhouse* called *The Facts Speak For Themselves* by Mark Leech, a former prisoner who had been released and written about his experiences. Perhaps my favourite was an episode of Michael McStay's detective series *Coleman and Astor* where (spoilers!) I played the villain in an episode called *A Day at the Races*. My main memory of this one is that after the read-through and before we were to record, the director said to me, "You do know that you are supposed to be Scottish in this?" I hadn't a clue, so with no further rehearsal, I gave them my best Glaswegian twang and apparently got away with it; I know this because when Liz heard the play, she didn't realise it was me!

However, by the late 1990s, despite leaving Alec behind over five years previously, I was still working in his shadow. Outside of my appearances in *Sooty & Co*, the only other television role I got was in the comedy series *The Detectives*, though once again I would be playing, you guessed it, a police sergeant. I hope I don't sound too boastful when I say that I thought I was quite funny in this show. It was discussed that my character, Hawkeye, would come back for more episodes.

Unfortunately, Jasper Carrott and Robert Powell decided to hang up their handcuffs for good and not make another series. Just my luck! But I enjoyed my few days on it, especially having some nice scenes with George Sewell, with whom I had spent a couple of years in *Oh What A Lovely War*.

When it came to theatre work, because of the Z-list celebrity status that my association with the programme still afforded me, I was receiving straight offers to star in tours of plays around the country, where I was even billed as 'Sgt. Peters from *The Bill*'. I took this work basically because it paid a lot more than I ever got at Strafford East, but these productions weren't as professionally put together as I was used to. The one that sticks in my mind is a production of *And Then There Were None*, one of Agatha Christie's most famous stories. I was told we would be having one week's rehearsal before opening at the Grand Theatre in Swansea, a very nice theatre that had just celebrated its centenary. We were then going to take the play around the UK, touring for far too many weeks. The cast would have to sort their own digs out at each stop as well, and I did feel I was too old to be doing this.

I was asked to be at the Grand Theatre on Monday afternoon, which surprised me considering we only had a week's rehearsal and I didn't know any of the other actors. I duly arrived and no one seemed to know what was going on. Eventually, I met the other actors appearing in this masterpiece, including *Hi-De-Hi* stars Ruth Madoc and David Griffin, Eve Steele from *Coronation Street* and Jack Smethurst of *Love Thy Neighbour* fame. Having been told that the director would be with us soon, it wasn't until 5pm that he finally appeared, at which point he revealed that our rehearsals wouldn't begin until the next day! As if this wasn't frustrating enough, he said we would begin our company bonding by watching another production he was directing at the theatre that evening; the Joe Orton play *What the Butler Saw*, with my old Corona mate Frazer Hines in the lead role. The director also revealed that some of my co-stars were also appearing in *What the Butler Saw* and that they would need a rest after this performance, therefore we wouldn't begin rehearsing *And Then There Were None* until lunchtime the next day, but I was expected to come to rehearsals line-perfect. What had I agreed to?

I went into *What the Butler Saw* with limited expectations, as I knew this cast had only had a week's rehearsal as well. My God, imagine learning a Joe Orton play in just a week? Frazer had an enormous part in this play and was rarely off stage. With huge respect to him, I have no idea why he didn't walk off. The whole production was dreadful. I was now aware that ours wouldn't be any better on our first night, playing this very same venue with no doubt much of the same audience too, who probably turned up for every first night performance at their local theatre out of a sense of duty. I did wait to see Frazer in the bar afterwards and I gave him my opinion, which he totally agreed with, though ever the pro he had just soldiered on.

The next day we finally came to our first rehearsal, where the director gave us a talk and wanted to show us the model of the set that the designer had built. I have to admit, this was possibly one of the best models I had ever seen, with so much detail for the set, using the wallpaper and carpet that we would have on stage, working French windows and a couple of balconies. I noticed immediately that there were only two exits and I asked the director how this would work, as surely we would keep meeting each other as we walked to our deaths etc. It just isn't practical or believable to do a Christie with only two exits, but this director seemed to think it would be. It was now about 4pm and we still hadn't rehearsed a line yet. The director called a tea break, after which we finally ran Act One, doing our best not to bump into the furniture. That night at our digs, the cast shared their concerns at the lack of time and we decided to rehearse our lines together. Fortunately, in an Agatha Christie play, it really doesn't matter what you say, as long as the plot sort of makes sense.

I don't know how, but we managed to get through the first night and by the end of the week, we more or less knew the right words. I understood that the director was a good cricketer and played county cricket for Northamptonshire, which impressed me! Sadly his theatre skills weren't as good as his bowling; he couldn't have directed traffic. Also, he was having a relationship with our stage manager, who reported back to him any mutterings she overheard from the cast about his incompetence. I didn't know this at first, so I think I ended up in his bad books quite quickly.

I remember very little about the subsequent tour, except that we played at Belfast and Derry in Northern Ireland, both cities that were finally coming out of those terrible years of violence during the Troubles. In fact we were the first English touring company to play in Derry since the Troubles had ended earlier that year. Liz came over to be with me during this leg in Northern Ireland, as it was our 25th wedding anniversary and I hired a car so that we could drive around this lovely place during the daytime. I booked us in at The Beech Hill Country House Hotel, a lovely hostelry just outside Derry where we had a wonderful room overlooking the river and the city. We were told that our room was the very one that had been used in 1969 by Edward Kennedy, the

United States Senator who drove his car off Chappaquiddick bridge and fled the scene, while his passenger drowned. It was an eye opener for us to drive around the area and see some of the destruction after the Troubles, especially in Omagh where a car bomb had caused devastation only a couple of weeks before we arrived. A lovely part of the world, with such horrible memories.

I also recall we played at the Beck Theatre in Hayes, which sticks in my memory as dear Joan Littlewood turned up to see me in it. Thankfully, I didn't know she was in the audience until she came to see me backstage. She told me I was good, but the play was crap. Bless Joan, I think this was the last time I saw her too. She died in 2002 and I went to her funeral, which was attended by all the names you can think of in theatre. I think it was seeing Joan and knowing that she had seen me in this dreadful play that made me realise that I needed to rethink my career.

I had been going through a bad time in my decision-making, taking work that was well paid, but not up to the standard I had enjoyed before I joined *The Bill*. Never believe what you read about actors in a long-running series and what they earn. While you are in the series, you might be doing fairly well, but when you are out of work times can be tough. I have had my fair share of those times out of work and its one thing when you're young with no commitments, but when you have a mortgage to pay it's a case of "Don't panic Mr Mainwaring!" I was luckier than most as by this time, Liz's career had really taken off. She had left Thames after five years and gone freelance, a brilliant decision that got her lots of work in films. Sometimes she would work away and we wouldn't see each other for months, though if I was ever out of work I could go and visit her, and vice versa. Liz's knowledge of costume really is second to none and over the years she has worked on major series like *The Young Indiana Jones Chronicles* and *Band of Brothers*, to huge blockbusters like the *Pirates of the Caribbean* movies and *Captain America: The First Avenger*.

Thanks to the combination of Liz's success and my being sensible with my modest salary on *The Bill*, we were able to pay off our mortgage before the turn of the millennium. This meant that I could start to be more selective about the type of work I was doing. I had been working in showbiz for over 50 years - that's a very good innings for any actor and I felt I had nothing left to prove. But rather than retire, I decided to seek out work with young filmmakers and new playwrights, as a chance to work with the next generation and hopefully give something back. The strength of any profession starts at the bottom, which I think is very rarely appreciated.

The first project came in 1999, when I was cast to play the lead in a short film called *Drive*, made by Raina Haig for the Northern Film School. Raina was a granddaughter of Field Marshal Douglas Haig, commander of the British Expeditionary Force on the Western Front during the First World War. Shot in Yorkshire, in black and white, *Drive* told the story of a married couple driving through a bleak landscape on their way to visit their son's grave. Things become fraught on the journey and their relationship gradually disintegrates. Raina is partially sighted and watched the monitor with her nose almost touching the screen. *Drive* earned itself a place in film history, as it was the first ever fiction film to have audio description integrated at production stage, an innovation that deservedly earned Raina an award at Canada's Picture This Film Festival for 'The Best Contribution to Disability Culture'.

AN ACTOR RETIRES...

My experience on *Drive* really got my creative juices going again. It was the first of several short films I made, with a comedy following later the same year called *School Fête*, then another quirky one called *Plastic*.

I enjoyed working with young filmmakers, though theatre was still my first love. For me there is nothing like feeling the atmosphere created by being on stage and getting feedback from your audience, and I have been very fortunate to have felt this many times working with some of the best. But after all those dreadful tours that my Z-list celebrity had earned me, I was very keen for an opportunity to flex my muscles in a new play. My chance came in 2000, when I was attending a Hampton FC match. I was and remain a fan of this non-league side and a fellow supporter is actor Steve Morley, who played semi-regular Sergeant Stuart Lamont in *The Bill* for 12 years.

I knew that Steve was also a playwright and it was great to reconnect with him again at Hampton. During one match we started talking about 'the business' and I asked him what had been the key to him deciding to start writing as well as being an actor. He told me that whilst he was studying at Leeds University in the 1970s, he went to see a production of *Waiting For Godot* that had made a great impression on him. I wondered whether this had been the same production that I had been in and we worked out that it was! All the time we knew each other on *The Bill* and we hadn't realised our connection. I must say I felt great about being part of such a positive influence for Steve and it was a reminder of the kind of theatre I missed doing.

I was absolutely delighted when in 2000 Steve asked me to play the lead in his new historical fantasy *The Jests of*

Skoggan, which is told through flashback and before a backdrop of the Wars of the Roses. My character of John Skoggan is now an old man who recounts his epic tales of being court jester to King Edward IV to an emissary of France, who has been sent to find out if the tales are true. Forever on the lookout for a jest so that they might laugh and fare well, Skoggan and his old friend William sing, dance and blunder their way through medieval England, at a time when "England was truly merry". We performed at the Rose & Crown pub theatre in Hampton Wick and it turned out to be very successful. Whilst the venue only had 50 seats, the queues for returns throughout our four-week run were long and many were disappointed at not being able to see it. I don't often blow my own trumpet, but I got the best reviews of my career, with The Stage declaring that I gave a "wonderful performance" and similarly What's On magazine described my Skoggan as "magnificent." I was back.

The following year, Steve was keen to try out his next play at the same venue and once again he invited me to play the lead. This time he created an extraordinary one-act play called *Zoo*, set three years after the collapse of the Soviet Union. This political piece also needed a leading lady to play the wife of my zookeeper, who eventually gets killed by one of the tigers. I recommended my great mate Melody Kaye, sister to my agent Kap and a super actor. We had worked together many times with Ken Hill at Stratford East, most memorably on *The Last Of The Dinosaurs*. Mel was great as usual and we enjoyed another successful four-week run at the Rose and Crown. I'm very grateful to Steve for reigniting my love for the theatre through his plays. I'd have loved to do them for longer.

AN ACTOR RETIRES...

Then in 2002, an actor called Paul Jerricho, with whom I played a lot of cricket for Chadwick, asked me to be in his production of Alan Bennett's *Talking Heads* at the New Wimbledon Theatre. Paul was putting on three of these wonderful thirty-minute monologues and asked me to play the role of Graham Whittaker in *A Chip in the Sugar*, a wonderful part that Bennett himself had played and won a BAFTA. I could hear his voice as I performed it. The writing was so good and Paul did such a great job of directing all three plays that we honestly should have gone on tour and performed them around the country. I am very proud of the work we all did on these productions.

I was still keeping my hand in with more mainstream work for Kap, including a number of pantomimes thanks to my continuing Z-list status from *The Bill*! These productions were obviously not challenging, but they were fun to do for quite a few Christmases. I think I have been an Ugly Sister four times, a Dame once and King Rat (the best part) a couple of times. But I did at least feel I had found the right balance through the plays I had done with Steve and Paul, and I started to wonder if perhaps this was the right time to retire. But then, along came *EastEnders*...

The director Michael Owen Morris was a mate of mine who I played cricket with, as well as golf and occasionally bowls. In 2007, he offered me a part in two episodes of *EastEnders* that he was directing. I was to play a man called Brian, a reporter from the local newspaper. Michael was a leading director on the series, and it was his hope that this character could then make semi-regular appearances whenever the storylines needed, which would have suited me nicely at this stage of my career.

I had always wanted to avoid joining a soap, as I didn't

want to be tied down as an actor. The closest I came was in 1960, when I went to Manchester to record a pilot for a new soap called *Florizel Street*. I was to play the part of Dennis Tanner and as it was a pilot, the fee was tiny and I had to cover my accommodation for a week. I agreed to share a room in a hotel just up the road from the studio with another actor, called William Roache! This soap would of course go on to be called *Coronation Street*, though my part was recast after the pilot and would be played by Philip Lowrie, who was much better than me as he was a proper Lancastrian. I wasn't too upset about this, as work was coming along thick and fast at the time, though I must admit that I was disappointed that Granada hadn't told me. In fact, I had to find out by watching the telly and realising I could still recite all of Dennis Tanner's dialogue. I can't believe that at the time of writing, Bill Roache is still playing Ken Barlow all these years later!

Fast-forward nearly 50 years to my first day on Albert Square, where I had to begin by photographing one of the regular characters, Chelsea Fox (played by Tiana Benjamin) whilst she was being arrested. During this shot, Michael gave me licence to improvise as I took photos of her being escorted out of the Queen Vic and being put in the back of a police car. Sounds simple, but I soon found myself being made to feel quite uncomfortable. It became clear to me that some of the younger members of the regular cast were thinking, "who is this extra imposing himself in this scene?" Not one of them introduced themselves to me, which was something that all of us on *The Bill* prided ourselves in doing when new actors arrived on our set. Any actor going into an established show is usually a little unsettled by the occasion, and so naturally we as a company wouldn't want to impose this feeling on our guest actors. Sadly,

AN ACTOR RETIRES...

this didn't appear to be the ethos on *EastEnders*. At the end of this shot, I was released, as I wouldn't be needed again until the next day to shoot the interiors of the Queen Vic in studio.

The second day got off to a much happier start, as on arriving the first person I saw was Rudolph Walker, a great actor who I had worked with a couple of times, including when he won the Evening Standard's Best Actor award for his work on the play *King of England* at E15. Also, just before I got to my dressing room, I bumped into Phil Daniels, who I knew socially, and thankfully we were to have a scene together.

On set whilst waiting for Michael Owen Morris to arrive, I noticed that once again all the younger cast members kept their distance. That all changed when suddenly I heard a loud voice shout "Larry!" It was Barbara Windsor, who appeared from behind the bar. She was not in this episode, but had left something on the set the previous day and had come to collect it. Barbara rushed over and gave me a big hug. We then had a lovely chat until Michael arrived to start work. Suddenly the attitude of the younger cast members, who had been less than polite to me, totally changed. The amazing power of Barbara Windsor's influence; what a wonderful lady, and now so sadly missed. I then recorded my scenes, including a nice one with Phil Daniels, and then went home. To be honest, I was glad to get away and perhaps it was for the best that my character was never reintroduced! However, I didn't feel I could retire with this rather short-lived outing in *EastEnders* and kept my eyes peeled for one last hurrah.

My prayers were answered in 2010, when I was cast in a production of *The Ragged Trousered Philanthropists*. This three-month engagement felt like the perfect full-circle for me, as I had been in the 1968 version made for television, directed by

Christopher Morahan. Christopher was back to direct this stage version and he cast me to play the wonderful part of Old Joe Philpot. All the younger members of the cast wanted to know how it was working with Christopher, as he had a reputation for being a hard taskmaster. In fact, as he was now 80, he had softened a lot since the last time I had worked with him and I found him great to work with and his notes were always to the point.

For this production, we were playing six weeks at the Everyman Theatre in Liverpool, followed by another six weeks at the Minerva Theatre in Chichester. I hoped that the production would organise some decent digs for us to stay in for this length of time, and how lucky was I! In Liverpool I had digs with a lady called Terry, who had two lovely dogs that I could take out for walks for her. After a couple of weeks, Terry asked me if I would mind looking after the house while she was away for a week. Such trust! I really liked Liverpool and having never worked there before, it was great to spend my free time enjoying the museums and all that there is do there. I still hear from Terry on Facebook. Then in Chichester, I stayed with a lovely lady who always had a jigsaw on the go, which I was encouraged to help with whenever I wanted. In both digs, I was allowed to use the kitchen and cook for myself, which was great. I knew Chichester fairly well, as my late Aunt Jean had lived there with her husband John and family. I used to cycle there for the day in the Fifties and early Sixties; looking back now I am amazed that I ever did this, I must have pedalled 120 miles each trip!

I have really lovely memories of my time on *The Ragged Trousered Philanthropists*, especially working with Christopher and the fantastic cast he assembled, we worked brilliantly together.

AN ACTOR RETIRES...

Once again, I earned myself some nice words from the critics, including The Guardian who praised my "fine work as the elderly Joe." As the play is set in the early part of the twentieth century, most of the men had moustaches, and literally straight after the final curtain there was a fight to get to the sink in the dressing room and shave them off. I miss that cast. I made the decision that this would be my last time working in theatre, doing a job that I loved and going out with a little joy.

I was satisfied with my decision to retire, but then I was asked to do one last job by Kenneth Parrott, a theatre director I had worked with before, who had been sent a new play by a young writer called Robert Francis. He had asked for me specifically to be in this rehearsed reading in front of invited guests and, as Kenneth is very persuasive, I agreed to read the script. The play was called *Storming Out* and was a short piece about a young man telling his very working class parents that he was gay and the subsequent upheaval this causes. It became clear to me that this was Robert's own story, and I thought his script was very good. We were to perform this showcase at a small theatre in The Actors Centre, with Anna Carteret playing the mum and Robert playing our son. We did it in a day and I thought it went quite well.

I then thought no more about it until I got a call from Robert, saying that a filmmaker had seen the reading and wanted to make a short film based on the play. I met up with Robert and the director, Vito Bruno, who explained how it would all work. We would shoot in Manchester, using a house that Vito was sharing as our location, and whilst there was no fee for the actors, all our expenses would be covered. I drove up with Anna and we had two days filming with Vito and his really good crew and we got it done. I then drove Anna back to my house, where her husband Christopher Morahan was waiting for her. It was great to see him again after *The Ragged Trousered Philanthropists*, and Liz was very impressed that this important director was at our house!

Robert sent me a copy of the finished film, which I enjoyed and hoped it would be lead to bigger things for he and Vito. In fact, Robert later phoned me to tell me that *Storming Out* had won first prize at a film festival in the USA! Well done Robert and Vito, who went onto become a leading first assistant director in television, as well as occasionally directing series himself. In fact, in 2016 he got me a couple of episodes in the children's BBC series *Twirlywoos*. Thanks Vito!

So faithful reader, having tried to bow out gracefully several times, have I now finally hung up my boots and retired? Well, yes I have and I did it in a way that amused me, which I have kept a secret until now! In 2021, when my friend Michael Owen Morris was asked to do his last ever episode of *EastEnders* after many years, I asked him if I could be in it, as an extra very much in the background. I didn't want to be paid, I just thought it would be fun. He said he could find a place for me in a park scene, where I could easily be put in the background. He asked if I could find someone to sit with me at a table drinking a cup of tea. I asked Melody if she wanted to do this and she was of course delighted. We got to the studios at Elstree, where Mike arranged visitor passes for us, as we were not there officially as actors. We did our little cameo scene, had a spot of lunch with Mike and then we left. For me, this was a fun and silly way of leaving the business. I started off as a child extra and, after a career spanning over 70 years, I would leave the business as an 80-year-old extra. Mel and I often have lots of laughs about our award-winning performances as tea-drinking extras.

CHAPTER 21

The Golden Years

We always wanted to have a family together. I wanted two kids, one of each. I always joked that I would call the boy either Neil Dann, Ben Dann or Sid Dann... this didn't go down well with Liz. We practiced a lot to have a baby, but without any success and it came to the point when we felt we needed to see our doctor for help. He got us a session at the NHS Infertility Clinic at Ashford Hospital. But for some reason I was never allowed into the room with Liz for discussions, and the whole process became rather spasmodic; weeks would pass between visits and Liz said she never saw the same doctor twice. In the end, it was a total waste of time. Fortunately, Liz was working with a girl who had just gone through the whole process at a private hospital in Chelsea. She gave us the details of who to contact.

We met our clinician, Mr Edmunds, who talked us through the whole process. This was already so much better, as we were both part of the discussions. IVF treatment would cost us £2,000. We agreed to go ahead, but poor Liz had to go through so much. We had to time it for when Liz was at her cycle and have sex first thing in the morning, then rush to the hospital in Chelsea for Liz to go through heavens knows what. This happened a few times, then Mr Edmunds said they had enough samples from us both and we could go forward with the implant. They implanted the fertilised egg back into Liz and then we would wait...

After three weeks, we went back for a scan to find out if the egg was growing. Sadly it wasn't, it had gone. I felt dreadful and I have no idea how much more pain Liz must have felt. We had an inquest with Mr Edmunds, who said that we could have another try as he felt there was no real reason why it should fail again. We agreed to try again and invested another £2,000. This time we didn't have to go through all the same preamble from the first time as they still had enough of Liz's eggs to plant three more... perhaps we would end up with triplets? Take 2, and this time we saw that the egg was there and growing! We came back the next day and all was going well, with the Brazilian doctor who was in charge of the scan saying he believed it had worked. "See you tomorrow." Our hopes were high!

Tomorrow came, but this time the scan showed nothing, the egg had gone. Disaster. That is without doubt the lowest I have ever felt in my life. Mr Edmunds told us that the only thing wrong was that "we didn't have the glue." I didn't want Liz to go through all this again and she felt very much the same. We decided to enquire about adoption, but at 40 years of age, I was told that I was too old to adopt! That was the law at the time in 1981.

It was around this time that we decided to put our home in Hanworth on the market. We had now lived there for seven years and done lots of work to make it lovely. And whilst we weren't moving to have a family, we felt our successful careers meant that we could afford to get something more upmarket.

We put the house on with a local estate agent for £27,000 and we worked out that we could go to £45,000 with a £15,000 mortgage. Literally on the first day of being advertised, a young couple came to see our house and immediately wanted to give us a deposit of £50 pounds on the spot. Now all we had to do was find our new property... Needless to say, we found it hard to find what we wanted. It seemed like the more we looked, the less we saw. After about six months of searching, the young couple told us that they had to move in very soon, as they had sold their place and were ready to go. Panic stations! We decided to take a house we had seen in Hampton, priced at £45,000, exactly the amount we wanted to pay. We gave the estate agent the deposit of £500 and started the ball rolling by putting in a surveyor to check the place out.

That weekend, we were to go up to Durham as Liz's cousin Philip was getting married on the Sunday. On the Friday night before travelling up to Durham, I got a phone call that I will never forget. "Hello Mr Dann, you don't know me, but my name is Mr Nickols. I am the surveyor you sent to see the house you are about to buy. I advise you NOT to proceed as that house has many problems, subsidence, dry rot, broken drains..." The list was endless! Now we were in real trouble, as we had to get out of our house in two weeks and now we had nowhere to go, plus we were supposed to be leaving for Durham first thing in the morning.

I got up early and went to the estate agent to cancel and retrieve our deposit. I then started to visit all the local agents to get our names down for anything. The first agent I went to see was Martingale and Knight on Hampton Hill High Street. I remember the agent's first words were, "What are you doing here, I thought you had bought a house?" When I explained what had happened, she immediately took me by the hand and walked me to a house right opposite the shop, a large Edwardian halls-adjoining semi, with a driveway off the street. She took me inside and I got that instant feeling when you know a place is right for you, but I knew I wouldn't be able to afford it. The agent explained that it was sold, but just before I came in that morning the man who was buying it had pulled out, having got home the previous night to find his wife in bed with someone else! The agent then said it was on the market for £60,000, but that the owners were in financial trouble and had just authorised her to sell for £45,000! I couldn't believe it. I explained that I really wanted this house, but that I must get Liz to come and look at it too. We came back twenty minutes later with our brand new puppy, Gimli, and Liz couldn't believe it either. We agreed to buy, put the deposit down and then headed off to Durham. What amazing luck!

The house had belonged to a garage just a few doors up the road, which also had a campervan rental scheme. They used the house for clients to stay in whilst they prepared for their holiday. It was sold with a 150ft garden that was totally overgrown, in fact you really couldn't see further than about 20ft from the back door. It took me four weeks of cutting back, and a bonfire that never went out during the whole time. My new neighbours were not too happy about this, but they understood my mission. During my hacking through the jungle, I found the remains of an old car, complete with rusty old chassis, flat tyres and worn-out seats. It took many trips to the recycling yard to get rid of this vehicle, but when you're an out of work actor it's good to have a project to keep you going!

It was all worth it in the end and we had a really good garden where many a barbecue was enjoyed.

This house was a joy to live in, with all the shops we needed on the quiet high street, with very little through traffic and plenty of pubs within walking distance. Sadly, over the years it became much busier with traffic and the limited parking meant that so often we would find people parking across our drive to visit the shops or, worst of all, for an appointment at the the ladies' hairdressers opposite! Many a time Liz would go over and ask who owned the car ABC 123 and would get a reply, "It's me, I'll only be twenty minutes."

Then in 2002, our lives were to change again. We had a knock on the door from an unpleasant housing developer, who wanted to buy our house and the one next to us, along with the block of eight flats to our left. I think they wanted to build 40 flats and it hadn't taken them long to get permission from the council. Now all they needed was permission from the owners of these properties. I know that all the occupants in the flats agreed a fee to leave, while the lady who owned next door, and had made her house into three units, agreed and sold up. We were in the middle of the development and were offered about £550,000, which sounds a lot, but at the time we had our house valued at £475,000. We declined, especially as we both took a dislike to the slimy man who first approached us and we told the developing company that we didn't want this person to come to our house again. Before we knew it, along came the CEO himself, who went on the full charm offensive - he really needed our house! Liz was very firm and told him that we really didn't want to leave. We were told that the build would go ahead without us and that we would be left surrounded by the new constructions, which of course we knew could never happen.

Six years later, we were offered a price that we would never have got without Liz's firmness. We got over twice the price it was valued at and our little £45,000 house made us millionaires! How unbelievably lucky, and I would like to personally thank the lady who had an affair and enabled us to buy the house. As they say, it's all in the timing! This meant that we could afford to buy our current house overlooking the River Thames in Sunbury.

We would have obviously preferred to have children, but I suppose being childless meant that for the rest of our lives we could afford to treat ourselves to some lovely holidays. Though as you will recall from my escapades on *Maybury*, if something can go wrong on the organisational front, it usually does when I am concerned! For example, I once had two weeks off from *The Bill* and so we booked a trip to Turkey with some friends. We spent our first week sailing up the Turkish coast on a gulet from Fethiye and then onto Olu Deniz to spend our second week on the beach. After a couple of days sunbathing, I thought it would be wise for me to look at the script for my next episode, which I would be filming on my return. Imagine my shock when I noticed that the first filming day listed on the front of the script was in three days' time, and our return flight wasn't until the day after! I had to get back to London!

The only problem was that we were on a charter flight from Dalaman Airport and there weren't any more available to London. I was advised to get to the next closest international airport in Izmir, some 200 miles away! How would I get there? I was told there was a coach station in the square outside and sure enough, I found a plethora of options. I chose a Mercedes coach and found out it would cost just £1.50 to take me on my 200-mile trip, complete with air conditioning and cool water supplied at no charge. Result! I said my goodbyes to Liz, who stayed on with the gang to enjoy the rest of our holiday as planned. About five hours later, I arrived at Izmir and got a taxi to the airport, where I got a BA flight to Heathrow. I was saved! I arrived back in London with a day to freshen up before filming my next episode. That little holiday certainly wasn't as cheap as I'd planned, though you can imagine how much more expensive it would have been had I not checked that script. I'd have been in real trouble!

After my Dad died in 1993, a friend of my brother Ian kindly offered us all the use of his apartment near Faro in Portugal, which he recommended if we fancied getting away for a break and a spot of golf. Along with our brother John, that's exactly what Ian, Liz and I decided to do. Our good friend Mandy's daughter Polly worked in a travel agent and got us a very good price on return flights to Faro, and we booked a car to get around for the week. We had excellent weather, ate well and played some good golf as we talked about Dad. Everything worked brilliantly... until it was time to come back!

We arrived in plenty of time for our 8pm flight, only to find that the airport was completely empty. We even managed to park right outside the terminal - where was everybody? Proceeding inside, we could only find one man wandering about. We asked him why it was so quiet and his reply made my blood run cold. "All flights today are gone." We checked our tickets to make sure we had the right time, and printed in exceedingly small writing was a notice that we were booked on a charter flight, which we'd needed to phone in advance to confirm! We hadn't done this and the flight had left some three hours earlier, meaning the four of us were now stranded in Faro Airport without lodgings for the night. Fortunately, we still had the hire car and we drove back to the apartment, though we had of course already given the keys back. Thankfully we found the caretaker and begged him to let us have the keys back for the evening, which he did.

The next day, we left very early in the morning to go back to the airport and buy tickets for a flight home, only to be told there was a queue for returns, as Faro was now operating charter flights only. Unless we waited, we would have to go to Lisbon and try from there! Hours passed and it was mid-afternoon by the time we were first in line. A flight to London was available, but with only one seat. We told Liz to take it, so at least she would get home, but ten minutes later she was back, as the person whose ticket this was had arrived at the departure gate just before she was about to get on. It was teatime when we were told there were finally four seats available, but the flight was going to Manchester. We took it, otherwise I think we would still be at Faro Airport!

My amazing organisational skills were in full flow for Liz's 50th birthday, when I took her to a lovely town in the snowy mountains of Norway called Geilo. We stayed at the exceptional Geilo Mountain Lodge, which I booked by fax. As well as being a popular ski resort, Liz's main present was the opportunity to go dog sledding! This came with a surprise for me too, as I thought we would be driven by an experienced hand… but no, we were to drive the dogs ourselves! We were given one simple lesson, "Do not fall off, because the dogs do not stop!" It turned out to be fantastic fun, especially as the dogs knew the route off by heart, they were basically on autopilot! Everyone should try it.

The next day, after our usual ski run back to the hotel, we found all our cases and belongings stacked up in the foyer. I went to the desk and demanded to know what was going on, as we weren't due to leave until the next day. It was then the receptionist produced my fax and pointed out that I had booked for us to check out that very day. They'd had to remove all our belongings while we were out skiing, as their next guests were due to arrive and the rest of their double rooms were fully booked. I did my best pathetic apology routine and asked if they could squeeze us in anywhere? They found us the smallest single room you can imagine, and an extremely expensive one at that, but it was either that or a long train ride to Oslo Airport!

But our great holiday love is cruising, which all began thanks to a huge slice of luck. Thanks once again to dear old Alec Peters, I was invited to the Water Rats' Ball at the Criterion Hotel in Park Lane, one of their big charity events. The room was full of about a thousand paying guests, and each table had a celebrity guest to keep them entertained. As Liz and I hadn't paid for a ticket, and we were getting a free meal and the occasional glass of wine, it felt almost obligatory to buy tickets for the raffle. I'd never won at a raffle and expected that if I did, the prize would probably be the usual out-of-date can of tomato soup! But the moment came and I duly paid my £20 for a ticket.

My old mate Gorden Kaye was King Rat, and he had gathered a lot of the stars of his very funny show 'Allo 'Allo! to help him pick the winning numbers. It was Vicki Michelle who was invited up to pull out the first prize... and unbelievably it was my number. I wasn't really paying too much attention as Vicki came over to hand me the winning envelope. I nudged Liz who was chatting away and not even aware that I had bought a ticket, let alone that it had won first prize. I showed her the mystery envelope, still not knowing what was inside, and opened it... 'YOU HAVE WON A TWO-WEEK CRUISE WITH FRED OLSEN LINES'. We couldn't believe it, we had never even thought about going on a cruise! There was a brochure showing where we could go; the one proviso being that it had to be port to port.

We chose a Black Watch cruise from Dover around the Mediterranean, calling in at Lisbon, Malaga, Corsica and Nice. What I remember being struck by most was that there was always something to do on board whilst you were travelling to the next port, with good entertainment and plenty of food whenever you wanted. It also didn't really feel like we were at sea, as the ship seemed to glide through the waves. That was until we went through the Bay of Biscay. We were watching the evening cabaret when suddenly the ship started to rock and roll, literally! The magician had problems with his doves and the poor girl dancers had to give up. Quite a few of the elderly passengers began to panic, but the comic Jeff Stevenson was absolutely brilliant at keeping everyone calm, telling lots of gags around the situation, sadly none of which I can remember now. I can say that this was the first and only time we ever experienced a bumpy ride like this.

Far from putting us off, Liz and I became hooked on cruising. My cousin Barbara heard about our adventure and asked if we would like to go with them on a trip to the Panama Canal. They were going with four friends, but two of them had to pull out and so we were offered a chance to buy their

THE GOLDEN YEARS

tickets. We couldn't wait for our second cruise! We were to fly out to Los Angeles to get to our ship and as I had a friend who worked at London Airport in cargo, I asked him if he could get us upgraded. The six of us got upgraded to First Class and I became quite popular that day!

We sailed down the Pacific coast of Mexico, calling at places like Acapulco, where we went to a sanctuary for helping turtles to survive the destruction of their habitats due to population increase. We were each given a baby turtle to place in the sea, hoping they would one day make it back to have their own babies. Nature is very cruel to turtles and so few make it, though I'm convinced mine did. We then went to Costa Rica, where I could easily have lived. This was the only port on our trip where we weren't besieged by sellers of useless souvenirs that you would never give to your worst enemy! A few hundred yards away, we found a quiet little street market, where no one played the hard sell. And what did we do? We happily browsed and bought some gifts. There's a lesson there.

We also took a boat trip to see the local wildlife, which was amazing, like being in your own personal zoo, but without the cages. Exotic birds like toucans, parrots and spoonbills, up close and personal. I even saw a crocodile coming up out of its den. It could have only been a half-hour trip, but it was just amazing. We saw even more wildlife as we sailed through the Panama Canal, which was quite remarkable. This is where I saw my first sloth, lazing its way through the trees. The canal system works by using the replacement of water on a giant scale, simple physics I'm led to believe, but I still don't fully understand it! We then travelled to Cartagena, a port city on Colombia's coast. Cartagena is such a beautiful place to visit that it's hard to believe that it has so many problems with gangs and drugs.

We finished up our second cruise adventure by getting to our final destination in Miami, where we were to get our flight back home. On arrival, we were detained at a hotel just outside the airport, thanks to a volcano that had erupted in Iceland making it unsafe to fly. Fortunately it was only a four- or five-hour wait for us, but there was another family who had literally been waiting for days. We were lucky.

We have enjoyed many more cruises over the years, sometimes with Barbara and her husband Philip, or sometimes on our own. We've been to Alaska via Vancouver and the Rocky Mountains, Venice via Spain, Greece and Croatia. I'd be pushed to name a favourite, though it was possibly when we went to Burma, now known as Myanmar. We sailed the Irrawaddy River on a beautiful wood-panelled vessel with just 40 other passengers, mostly Aussies, who teased me mercilessly because we had just lost the Ashes. Or maybe the journey we took to the Galapagos via Quito in Ecuador was my favourite? Words can't describe the wildlife there, an island paradise with animals that have no fear of humans. Or was it the trip to Antarctica via Buenos Aires, where we had an extraordinary encounter in Ushuaia, the most southerly town in the world. Ushuaia is the capital of an area known locally as the Malvinas, which the British refer to as the Falkland Islands. On entering the port, we saw a sign that said 'No British Ships Here'. Despite this, we went to a café for a coffee and a bun. There we met an old gentleman, who shook our hands and thanked us just for being there and leaving the conflict in the past. A super moment.

THE GOLDEN YEARS

There are other trips we have been lucky to enjoy and I can honestly say that every one of them has been wonderful. If you've never been cruising, all I'll say is "Go!" The one we are looking forward to as I write these final words is our upcoming trip to celebrate our fiftieth wedding anniversary. After a flight to New York, we will get on a small ship with about 300 passengers and the same number of crew, and enjoy the first class treatment as we travel up the east coast of the USA, then on to Canada and up the St Lawrence river, finishing in Quebec. This will probably be our last cruise, as we are steadily running out of pennies, but what a way to celebrate my golden years with Liz.

I've said it a few times in this book, but I'll repeat it one last time... How lucky am I?

Taking part in the Lord Mayor's Show in 2023 on the CCA Art Bus. The theme for the procession was "Musical Genre" and Liz designed our sheet music costumes. *(Author's Collection)*

Acknowledgements

I would like to thank Oliver Crocker from Devonfire Books for choosing to publish my autobiography and for all his help in jogging my memory and taking all my written ramblings and formatting them into some kind of order for this tome.

Huge thanks to Tessa Crocker for her proofreading skills; Frazer Hines, Sherrie Hewson, Ben Leach, Robert Ross and Gemma Ross for their support and encouragement; and Linda Regan and Brian Murphy for the very kind introduction to this book. I would also like to thank Mark Blythe, Paul Jackson, Marc Morris and Steve Morley for providing images for use throughout this book.

Last, but by no means least, I would like to thank Liz, for everything.

Other Titles Available

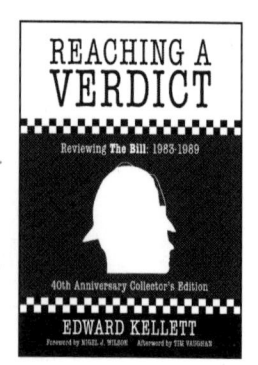

DEVONFIREBOOKS.COM